Solve the Riddles

Judy goes into the city to do some shopping.

Solve each riddle to determine how much money Judy has left when she returns home.

1. Judy has 5 dimes, 4 quarters, 4 $5 bills, and 1 $10 bill. How much money does she have?

_____

Judy buys some carrots for dinner. The carrots cost $12.50. How much money does she have left?

_____

2. Judy has 16 quarters and 3 $5 bills. How much money does she have?

_____

Judy spends $11 on a gift for her parents. How much money does she have left?

_____

3. Judy has 12 quarters and 1 $5 bill. How much money does she have?

_____

Judy buys a new book that costs $7.95. How much money does she have left?

_____

HINT First add the total amount of money Judy has to spend. Then subtract each item to determine how much she has left.

Fill In the Blanks

Ariel has many treasures in her secret grotto.
She keeps track of them all in her mind.

Use mental math strategies to determine each sum.

26 + 52 = _____

41 + 45 = _____

38 + 29 = _____

63 + 18 = _____

19 + 29 = _____

17 + 57 = _____

44 + 52 = _____

28 + 33 = _____

74 + 25 = _____

57 + 90 = _____

51 + 44 = _____

21 + 53 = _____

61 + 15 = _____

65 + 50 = _____

41 + 37 = _____

73 + 16 = _____

AWESOME!

HINT You can use the 100-chart on page 111 to help you.

22

Maze

Jacques wakes up Nemo at night. He tells Nemo to follow him to Mount Wannahockaloogie. There are two ways to get there.

Find two paths to the centre of the maze. Use your favourite mental math strategy to add the numbers along the path. Write the sum in the centre box.

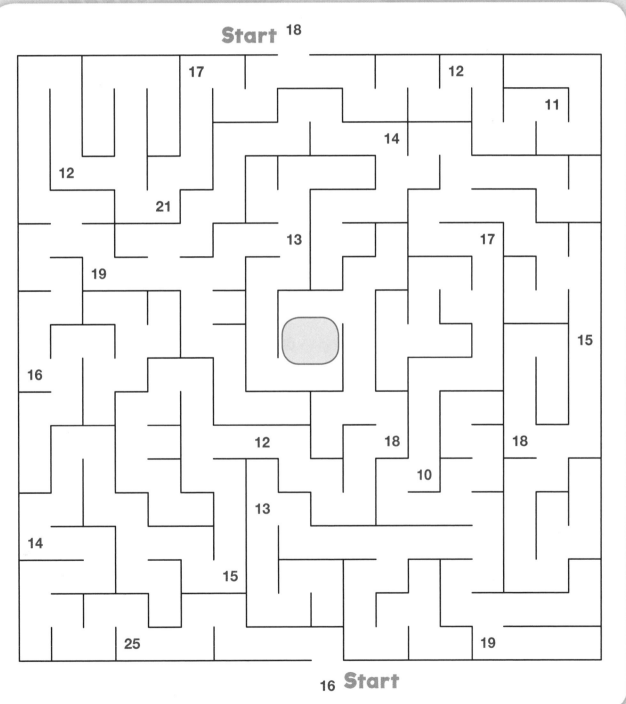

Crack the Code

Judy Hopps is studying for the math portion of her policing exam.
She reads a joke that makes her laugh out loud.

Use mental math strategies to determine each sum. Then use the letter that matches each sum to crack the code.

Letter Code

15 + 33 = _____ **T**   46 + 45 = _____ **L**

12 + 32 = _____ **P**   44 + 39 = _____ **O**

37 + 57 = _____ **M**   52 + 55 = _____ **F**

73 + 42 = _____ **U**   40 + 37 = _____ **S**

60 + 28 = _____ **A**   60 + 24 = _____ **B**

25 + 34 = _____ **E**   38 + 26 = _____ **V**

23 + 32 = _____ **D**   77 + 22 = _____ **R**

25 + 37 = _____ **Y**   18 + 35 = _____ **N**

Why was the math book sad?

Because it had _____ _____ _____   _____ _____ _____ _____
            48   83   83   94   88   53   62

_____ _____ _____ _____ _____ _____ _____ _____.
  44   99   83   84   91   59   94   77

Maze

The Beast has to find true love before the rose loses all its petals.

Find two paths to the centre of the maze.
Use mental math to subtract the numbers along each path.
Write the difference in the centre box.

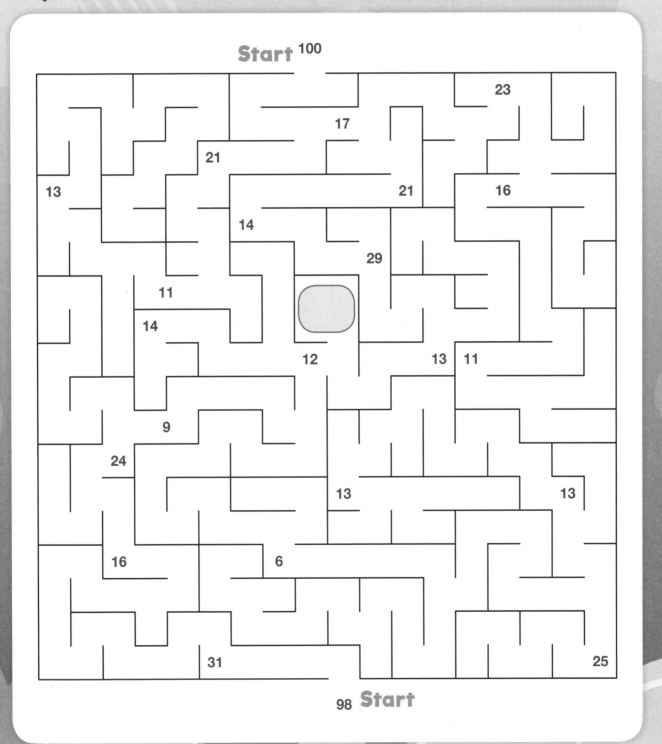

Start 100

23

17

21

13

21   16

14

21   16

14

29

11

14

12   13   11

9

24

13   13

16   6

31   25

98 **Start**

25

Crack the Code

Sometimes Beast eats too fast. What can happen if he eats too fast?

Use mental math strategies to determine each difference.
Then use the letter that matches each difference to crack the code.

NOM NOM

Letter Code

53 − 14 = _____ **A**

77 − 25 = _____ **C**

43 − 18 = _____ **E**

92 − 39 = _____ **H**

63 − 31 = _____ **I**

58 − 41 = _____ **M**

87 − 16 = _____ **O**

99 − 24 = _____ **P**

91 − 22 = _____ **R**

80 − 29 = _____ **T**

70 − 46 = _____ **U**

66 − 33 = _____ **Y**

What can happen if Beast eats too fast?

He can get a ____ ____ ____ ____ ____   ____ ____ ____ ____.
              51   24   17   17   33   39   52   53   25

#UH-OH

Fill In the Blanks

Andy is moving. As the moving boxes are packed up, they are taken away.
It's hard for Woody to keep track of how many boxes there are!

Use mental math strategies to determine each difference.

98 − 27 = _____   58 − 41 = _____

71 − 19 = _____   50 − 17 = _____

64 − 27 = _____   27 − 11 = _____

83 − 62 = _____   28 − 13 = _____

31 − 17 = _____   43 − 20 = _____

45 − 32 = _____   52 − 16 = _____

93 − 62 = _____   65 − 50 = _____

85 − 33 = _____   44 − 13 = _____

Crack the Code

Marlin and Dory know that friends are important.
Friends stick with you through thick and thin!

Determine each sum. Then use the letter that matches
each sum to crack the code.

Letter Code

```
  1128          3479          6350          3468
+ 6534        + 5521        + 2260        + 5486
```
     C   T   H   E

```
  1107          8348          1557          4932
+ 1578        + 1607        + 1884        + 4015
```
     O   M   N   U

Why do number lines make good friends?

Because you can always ___ ___ ___ ___ ___
                             7662 2685 8947 3441 9000

___ ___ ___ ___ ___ ___!
2685 3441   9000 8610 8954 9955

BFF

HINT You can use the place value chart on page 112 to help you.

Crossword

The monsters at Monsters, Inc. scare thousands of kids.
They collect thousands and thousands of screams!

Complete the crossword by completing each addition sentence.

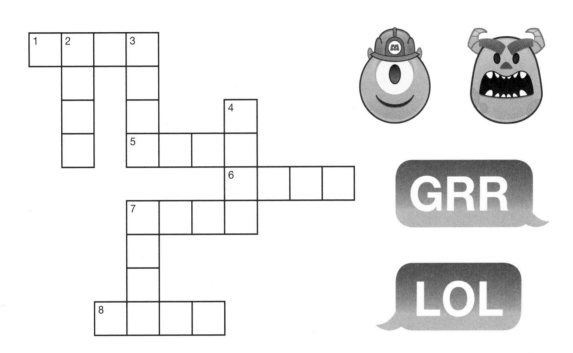

Across

1. 4563
    + 1171

5. 4322
    + 3508

6. 1872
    + 7109

7. 3440
    + 2923

8. 5802
    + 3310

Down

2. 1275
    + 6022

3. 2243
    + 2744

4. 2078
    + 1005

7. 4565
    + 1866

HINT Remember to regroup the ones, tens, or hundreds when the total is 10 or more.

Puzzle Pieces

Elsa creates thousands of snowflakes that cover the castle.

How many snowflakes does she create in total?
Use the puzzle pieces to complete each addition sentence.
Write the numbers in the answer boxes.

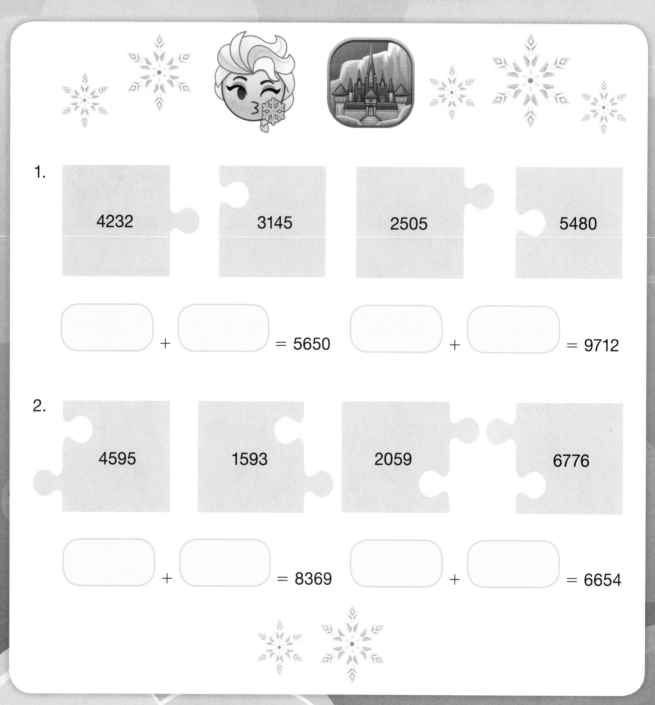

1.

| 4232 | 3145 | 2505 | 5480 |

[ ] + [ ] = 5650   [ ] + [ ] = 9712

2.

| 4595 | 1593 | 2059 | 6776 |

[ ] + [ ] = 8369   [ ] + [ ] = 6654

HINT Try different combinations of numbers to determine the total.

Crack the Code

Beast has a big problem to solve. How is he going to convince Belle to fall in love with him before all the rose petals fall off?

Determine each difference. Then use the letter that matches each difference to crack the code.

Letter Code

4011 − 1980	6782 − 2566	2000 − 1425	8143 − 4901	9000 − 3990
P	**Y**	**R**	**E**	**B**

5805 − 1092	8844 − 5928	6000 − 4725	2974 − 1899	8000 − 6994
M	**O**	**S**	**L**	**U**

What might a calculator say to Beast?

I'll solve _____ _____ _____ _____
 4216   2916   1006   575

_____ _____ _____ _____ _____ _____ _____ _____ .
2031   575   2916   5010   1075   3242   4713   1275

HINT You can use the place value chart on page 112 to help you.

31

Crossword

Dory swims thousands of kilometres to be reunited with her parents.
Each day, the distance she has to travel gets smaller and smaller.

Complete the crossword by completing each subtraction sentence.

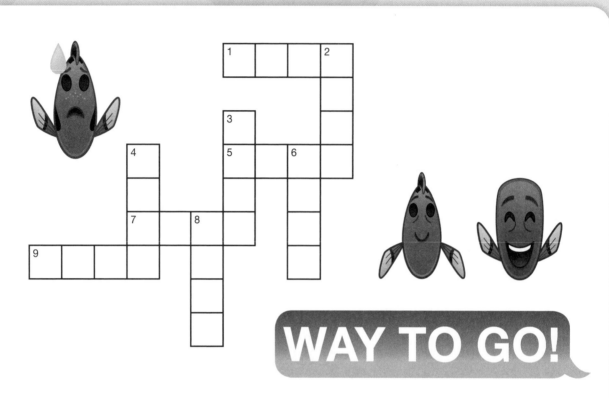

WAY TO GO!

Across

1. $\begin{array}{r} 7932 \\ -\ 5440 \\ \hline \end{array}$

5. $\begin{array}{r} 4799 \\ -\ 3177 \\ \hline \end{array}$

7. $\begin{array}{r} 6208 \\ -\ 3146 \\ \hline \end{array}$

9. $\begin{array}{r} 3570 \\ -\ 1671 \\ \hline \end{array}$

Down

2. $\begin{array}{r} 9174 \\ -\ 6542 \\ \hline \end{array}$

3. $\begin{array}{r} 2399 \\ -\ 1287 \\ \hline \end{array}$

4. $\begin{array}{r} 5552 \\ -\ 4113 \\ \hline \end{array}$

6. $\begin{array}{r} 3890 \\ -\ 1089 \\ \hline \end{array}$

8. $\begin{array}{r} 7676 \\ -\ 1254 \\ \hline \end{array}$

Fill In the Blanks

Mickey Mouse the Magician is trying some new magic.
He can make things disappear and reappear.

Some of the numbers have disappeared! Determine the missing number
for each subtraction sentence.

_____ − 4100 = 3400   _____ − 1000 = 8546

2300 − _____ = 1900   5645 − _____ = 3000

7921 − 4921 = _____   5829 − 829 = _____

_____ − 1025 = 5000   _____ − 5000 = 2437

8200 − _____ = 2800   9893 − _____ = 7000

4589 − 2000 = _____   7942 − 3942 = _____

_____ − 3466 = 5000   _____ − 1488 = 0

6710 − _____ = 2500   4315 − _____ = 2315

HINT When the first number in a subtraction sentence is
blank, add the other two numbers to determine the missing number.

33

Function Box

Some of the doors lead to rooms that have more than one child inside.
The monsters can collect two or three or more screams per door!

If Mike enters 3 doors and collects the same number of screams each time,
how many screams were collected at each door if the total is 12?

3 doors × ___4___ screams = 12 screams

Determine the missing number for each multiplication sentence.

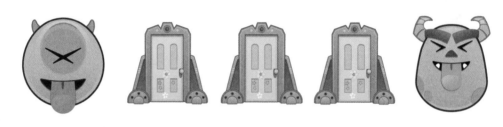

| 11 | × | = | 22 |

| | × 3 = | 18 |

| 7 | × 4 = | |

| 10 | × | = | 40 |

| | × 2 = | 20 |

| 7 | × 3 = | |

| 9 | × | = | 27 |

| 25 | × 4 = | |

| 8 | × 4 = | |

| 20 | × | = | 100 |

HINT You can check your answer using repeated
addition. For example, 10 × 3 is the same as 10 + 10 + 10.

Crack the Code

Cinderella does everything for her stepsisters. She might even have to do her stepsisters' math homework!

Determine each product. Then use the letter that matches each product to crack the code.

Letter Code

9 × 10 = _____ **T**   8 × 20 = _____ **L**

12 × 7 = _____ **E**   3 × 12 = _____ **S**

3 × 17 = _____ **M**   4 × 13 = _____ **D**

13 × 5 = _____ **A**   7 × 11 = _____ **O**

6 × 16 = _____ **U**   5 × 21 = _____ **B**

Why might someone do their multiplication homework while sitting on the floor?

Because they were told not _____ _____ _____ _____ _____
                            90   77   96   36   84

_____ _____ _____ _____ _____ _____.
 90   65   105   160   84   36

Function Box

Chief Bogo tells Judy to write 100 parking tickets. Judy is going to do even better than that! She will write two times as many parking tickets before noon!

Determine the missing number for each multiplication sentence.

☐ × 8 = 32   ☐ × 6 = 54

8 × 7 = ☐   7 × ☐ = 56

3 × ☐ = 24   9 × 8 = ☐

☐ × 7 = 28   ☐ × 8 = 40

5 × ☐ = 35   3 × 7 = ☐

HINT You can use the multiplication chart on page 112 to help you.

Fill In the Blanks

Aladdin and Jasmine are looking at the apples at the market. The apples are arranged in rows of equal length. They could use multiplication to determine the total number.

Determine each product.

17 × 3	16 × 6	13 × 4	13 × 6
14 × 8	12 × 7	11 × 6	20 × 6
20 × 8	11 × 9	15 × 4	12 × 9
10 × 8	19 × 5	14 × 8	18 × 3

Crack the Code

Goofy just saw someone eat their homework!
Why would anyone eat their homework?

Complete each division sentence.
Then use the letter that matches each quotient to crack the code.

Letter Code

12 ÷ 3 = _____ **O**   35 ÷ 5 = _____ **K**

8 ÷ 4 = _____ **I**   8 ÷ 8 = _____ **T**

30 ÷ 6 = _____ **E**   18 ÷ 6 = _____ **F**

27 ÷ 3 = _____ **C**   64 ÷ 8 = _____ **A**

24 ÷ 4 = _____ **P**   7 ÷ 7 = _____ **L**

Why would anyone eat their homework?

Because the teacher said it was a _____ _____ _____ _____ _____
                                      6   2   5   9   5

_____ _____ _____ _____ _____ _____.
  4   3   9   8   7   5

Function Box

The Little Green Aliens are going on a mission.
They divide themselves into groups.

Determine the missing number for each division sentence.

	÷ 3 =	3		32	÷ 4 =	
12	÷ 4 =			15	÷ =	3
24	÷ =	8			÷ 3 =	9
	÷ 5 =	9			÷ 4 =	3
24	÷ 4 =			40	÷ 5 =	
18	÷ =	6		27	÷ =	9
35	÷ 5 =				÷ 5 =	5

HINT Use multiplication to help you find the dividend.

39

Fill In the Blanks

Rapunzel loves looking at the lanterns in the sky.
She could use division to divide them evenly into groups.

Complete each division sentence.

63 ÷ 3 = _____   70 ÷ 5 = _____

52 ÷ 4 = _____   66 ÷ 2 = _____

44 ÷ 2 = _____   72 ÷ 6 = _____

75 ÷ 5 = _____   56 ÷ 4 = _____

66 ÷ 6 = _____   60 ÷ 3 = _____

36 ÷ 2 = _____   60 ÷ 5 = _____

80 ÷ 5 = _____   48 ÷ 2 = _____

90 ÷ 2 = _____   90 ÷ 5 = _____

65 ÷ 5 = _____   100 ÷ 2 = _____

GO LIVE YOUR DREAM!

HINT Multiply the quotient by the divisor to check your answer.

Function Box

While collecting garbage on Earth, Wall-E finds an old calculator.
He presses the buttons.

What numbers appear on the calculator? Determine the missing
number for each division sentence.

#WOW!

48	÷ 6 =	
	÷ 7 =	9
60	÷ ☐ =	10
88	÷ 8 =	
	÷ 6 =	16
35	÷ ☐ =	5
	÷ 8 =	5
42	÷ 7 =	

21	÷ 7 =	
54	÷ ☐ =	9
	÷ 8 =	12
72	÷ 6 =	
56	÷ ☐ =	7
	÷ 7 =	7
28	÷ 7 =	
60	÷ ☐ =	10

41

Picture Clues

Daisy Duck picks tulips from her garden.
She divides them into bunches.

Count the number of tulips. _____

How many groups of 5 tulips are there? _____

How many tulips are left over? _____

Write the division sentence. _____

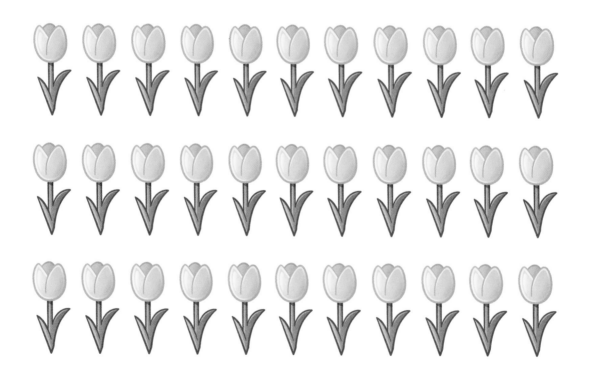

HINT Circle groups of 5 tulips. How many groups are there? How many tulips are left over?

Matching

Goofy is dividing everyone into soccer teams.
He wants the teams to be even so that no one is left out.

Determine how many people can be divided into how many teams.
Match each division statement to the remainders.

36 ÷ 8   remainder 1

44 ÷ 7   remainder 2

25 ÷ 9   remainder 3

30 ÷ 3   remainder 4

15 ÷ 2   remainder 5

23 ÷ 5   remainder 6

20 ÷ 7   remainder 7

50 ÷ 9   no remainder

FRIENDS 4EVER!

Fill In the Blanks

Moana and the islanders are collecting coconuts.
About how many coconuts do they collect?

Estimate each sum. Round each number first. Then add to estimate the sum.

133 + 94 = about _____

127 + 351 = about _____

274 + 459 = about _____

332 + 396 = about _____

622 + 288 = about _____

372 + 583 = about _____

175 + 180 = about _____

431 + 189 = about _____

114 + 190 = about _____

656 + 283 = about _____

229 + 318 = about _____

311 + 343 = about _____

219 + 632 = about _____

508 + 247 = about _____

592 + 381 = about _____

149 + 251 = about _____

291 + 479 = about _____

333 + 127 = about _____

HINT Round each number to the nearest hundred. Then add.

Fill In the Blanks

Sulley looks for Boo's door. But there are hundreds of doors in the factory! The doors get taken away by the hanging conveyor belts.

About how many doors are taken away? Estimate each difference. Round each number first. Then subtract to estimate the difference.

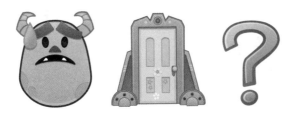

923 − 365 = about _____

742 − 601 = about _____

840 − 378 = about _____

785 − 194 = about _____

537 − 432 = about _____

926 − 456 = about _____

936 − 741 = about _____

791 − 541 = about _____

736 − 461 = about _____

476 − 119 = about _____

255 − 118 = about _____

722 − 598 = about _____

888 − 649 = about _____

902 − 156 = about _____

991 − 142 = about _____

820 − 287 = about _____

960 − 380 = about _____

408 − 179 = about _____

HINT Round each number to the nearest hundred. Then subtract.

Matching

Simba sees herds of different animals on the grasslands.
Each herd can have hundreds of animals.

About how many animals are there? Match each number in the
addition statement to the best estimate. The first one is done for you.

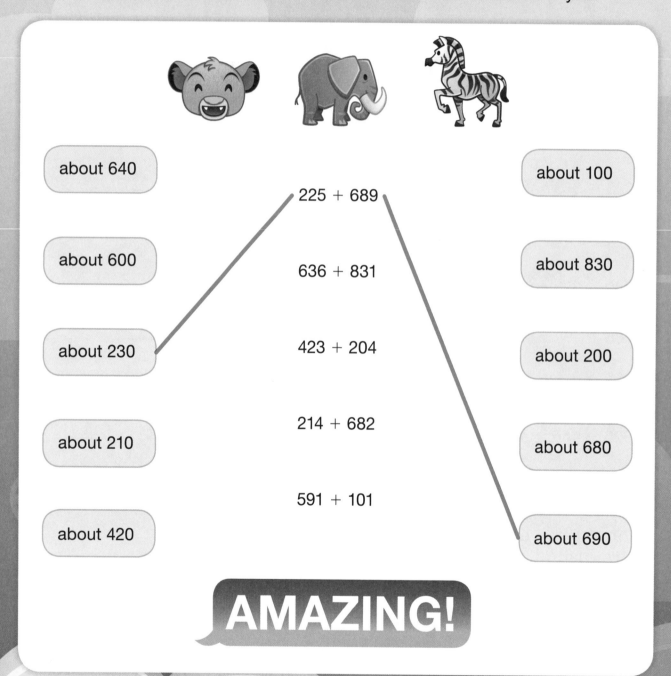

about 640

about 600

about 230

about 210

about 420

225 + 689

636 + 831

423 + 204

214 + 682

591 + 101

about 100

about 830

about 200

about 680

about 690

AMAZING!

HINT Look at the tens digit. If it is 5 or greater, round up.
If it is 4 or less, round down.

Fill In the Blanks

Genie uses magic to change objects from one thing to another.

You can use multiplication to change numbers.
Determine the product for each multiplication sentence.

$1 \times 10 =$ _____

$14 \times 10 =$ _____

$8 \times 10 =$ _____

$7 \times 10 =$ _____

$4 \times 10 =$ _____

$16 \times 10 =$ _____

How does the number change when you multiply it by 10?

_____

_____

$1 \times 100 =$ _____

$9 \times 100 =$ _____

$5 \times 100 =$ _____

$12 \times 100 =$ _____

$3 \times 100 =$ _____

$19 \times 100 =$ _____

How does the number change when you multiply it by 100?

_____

_____

HINT Look for a pattern when you multiply by 10 or 100.

Fill In the Blanks

Elsa does not want anyone to know about her ice powers. She's worried that thousands of people will find out at her coronation!

Fill in the blanks to show each number in its expanded form.

8793 = _____ thousands + _____ hundreds + _____ tens + _____ ones

2788 = _____ thousands + _____ hundreds + _____ tens + _____ ones

5478 = _____ thousands + _____ hundreds + _____ tens + _____ ones

3380 = _____ thousands + _____ hundreds + _____ tens + _____ ones

3509 = _____ thousands + _____ hundreds + _____ tens + _____ ones

7042 = _____ thousands + _____ hundreds + _____ tens + _____ ones

4286 = _____ thousands + _____ hundreds + _____ tens + _____ ones

9781 = _____ thousands + _____ hundreds + _____ tens + _____ ones

2007 = _____ thousands + _____ hundreds + _____ tens + _____ ones

HINT You can use the place value chart on page 112 to help you.

Matching

Mike and Sulley are in trouble. After Boo follows them into their world, their problems expand and get bigger and bigger!

Match each number to its expanded form.

8093   1 thousand + 8 hundreds + 5 ones

3761   5 thousands + 9 hundreds + 9 tens + 3 ones

2917   3 thousands + 7 hundreds + 6 tens + 1 one

1805   2 thousands + 8 hundreds + 1 ten

9122   8 thousands + 9 tens + 3 ones

7733   9 thousands + 1 hundred + 2 tens + 2 ones

2810   2 thousands + 9 hundreds + 1 ten + 7 ones

5993   7 thousands + 7 hundreds + 3 tens + 3 ones

#PROBLEMS

HINT In a 4-digit number, the first digit is the thousands, the second is the hundreds, the third is the tens, and the fourth is the ones.

Picture Clues

Moana and Pua go down to the beach.
While Moana looks out at the ocean, Pua sits in the shade.

Count the shaded parts of each picture. Determine the decimal value.

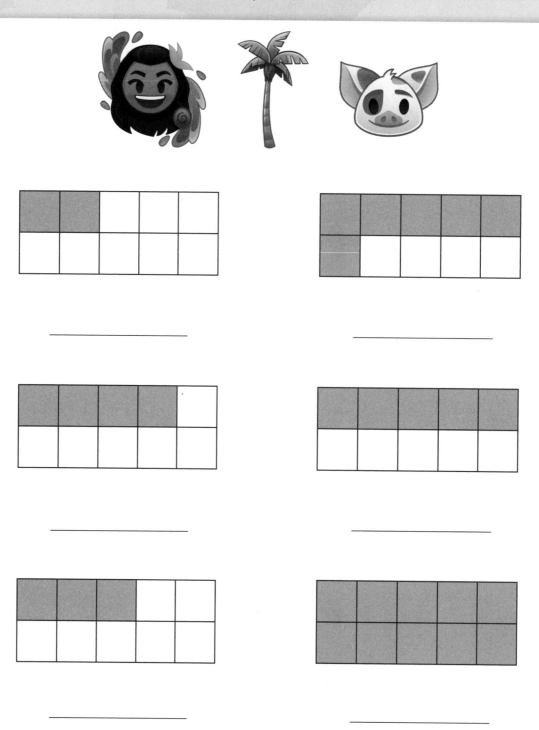

_____   _____

_____   _____

_____   _____

Puzzle Pieces

Cinderella has to put everything in order before she goes to bed.
Write these decimals in order from least to greatest.

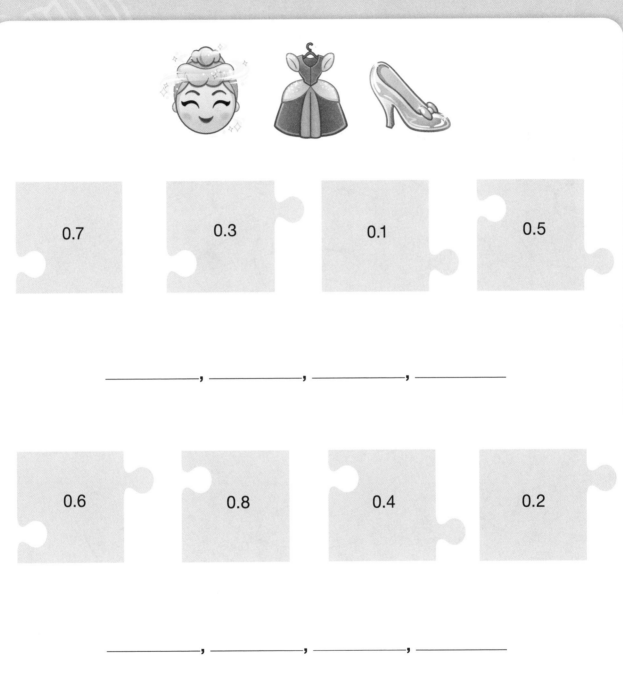

0.7   0.3   0.1   0.5

_____ , _____ , _____ , _____

0.6   0.8   0.4   0.2

_____ , _____ , _____ , _____

HINT The smaller the tenths digit, the smaller the decimal.

Maze

Jafar wants to be the greatest!
He will do whatever it takes to be the greatest.

Find your way through the maze.
Follow the numbers from least to greatest.

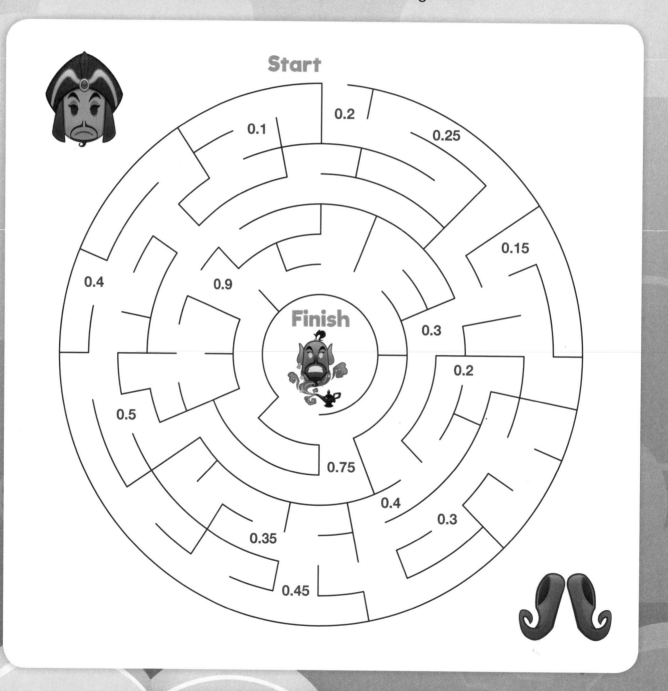

Start

0.2
0.25
0.1
0.15
0.4
0.9
0.3
Finish
0.2
0.5
0.75
0.4
0.3
0.35
0.45

HINT Compare the tenths and then the
hundredths digits to see which decimal is the greatest.

Crack the Code

Mickey told Minnie that he has a present for her.
But now he can't find it! He is nervous.

Write each fraction as a decimal.
Then write the letter that matches each decimal to crack the code.

Letter Code

A	E	H	N	O	S	T	W
$\frac{3}{5}$	$\frac{4}{10}$	$\frac{1}{10}$	$\frac{7}{10}$	$\frac{1}{5}$	$\frac{9}{10}$	$\frac{4}{5}$	$\frac{1}{2}$

Why couldn't the fraction relax?

It ____ ____ ____   ____ ____ ____
   0.5   0.6   0.9   0.8   0.5   0.2

____ ____ ____ ____ ____ ____ .
0.8   0.4   0.7   0.8   0.1   0.9

53

Matching

Marlin and Dory are racing through the jellyfish. They are competing to see who is fastest. They could measure their time to the nearest tenth of a second.

Match each decimal to the correct fraction.

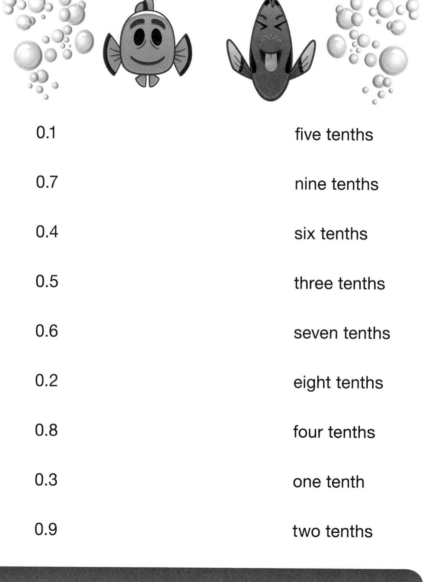

0.1	five tenths
0.7	nine tenths
0.4	six tenths
0.5	three tenths
0.6	seven tenths
0.2	eight tenths
0.8	four tenths
0.3	one tenth
0.9	two tenths

EAT MY BUBBLES!

HINT Say each decimal to hear the words.

Fill In the Blanks

Mickey and Minnie are baking together.
They have to convert the fractions in the recipe to decimals.

Write each fraction as a decimal.

$\frac{1}{5}$ = _____

$\frac{7}{10}$ = _____

$\frac{1}{2}$ = _____

$\frac{2}{5}$ = _____

$\frac{1}{10}$ = _____

$\frac{8}{10}$ = _____

$\frac{4}{5}$ = _____

$\frac{3}{5}$ = _____

$\frac{3}{10}$ = _____

$\frac{9}{10}$ = _____

$\frac{4}{10}$ = _____

$\frac{2}{10}$ = _____

WE'RE BAKING

YUM!

Fill In the Blanks

Mike likes his day to follow the same pattern: get up,
go to work, scare some children, go home.

Write the next 3 numbers in each number pattern.
Then write the pattern rule. The first one is done for you.

1. 2, 8, 14, __20__, __26__, __32__

   Pattern rule: Start at __2__ and ____increase____ by __6__ each time.

2. 3, 6, 12, _____, _____, _____

   Pattern rule: Start at _____ and _____ by _____ each time.

3. 58, 51, 44, _____, _____, _____

   Pattern rule: Start at _____and _____ by _____ each time.

4. 1, 6, 11, _____, _____, _____

   Pattern rule: Start at _____ and _____ by _____ each time.

 #LUVWORK

HINT You can add, subtract, or multiply to continue each pattern.

56

Fill In the Blanks

Mickey is trying to get his magic spell right.
More brooms appear, all carrying buckets of water!

Write the pattern rule for each number pattern.

1. 101, 107, 113, 119, 125, 131

   Pattern rule: Start at _____ and _____ by _____ each time.

2. 1, 3, 9, 27, 81, 243

   Pattern rule: Start at _____ and _____ by _____ each time.

3. 61, 56, 51, 46, 41, 36

   Pattern rule: Start at _____ and _____ by _____ each time.

4. 2, 4, 8, 16, 32, 64

   Pattern rule: Start at _____ and _____ by _____ each time.

Create your own number pattern.

_____, _____, _____, _____, _____, _____

Pattern rule: Start at _____ and _____ by _____ each time.

HINT Determine whether the pattern is increasing (addition or multiplication) or decreasing (subtraction).

Matching

Kristoff and Sven are loading the sleigh.
All the packages must be balanced, or else they'll fall off!

Equations must be balanced, too!
Match the equations so they are balanced.

15 + 24	1 × 5
15 ÷ 3	100 − 8
78 − 17	18 ÷ 3
2 × 3	10 + 9
37 + 55	40 − 1
81 − 62	60 + 1
81 ÷ 9	24 ÷ 4
6 × 1	3 × 3

LET'S GO!

HINT Solve each equation first. Then match the ones with the same answers.

58

Fill In the Blanks

Moana tries to balance four coconuts in her arms without any of them falling.

Can you keep four numbers balanced? Fill in the blanks to complete each equation. Both sides of the equation have to balance. Space is provided for you to show your work.

_____ × 5 = 10 ÷ 2

94 − _____ = 30 + 7

6 + _____ = 110 − 55

_____ ÷ 8 = 3 × 3

9 × _____ = 81 ÷ 9

12 ÷ _____ = 1 × 1

_____ − 122 = 200 + 10

_____ + 98 = 36 + 120

2 × _____ = 64 ÷ 8

56 ÷ _____ = 2 × 4

HINT Solve one side of the equation first. Then use multiplication and division facts to determine the missing value.

Function Box

Belle loves books. The bookstore in town does not have many books. The Beast has lots of books.

Complete each equation. The first one is done for you.

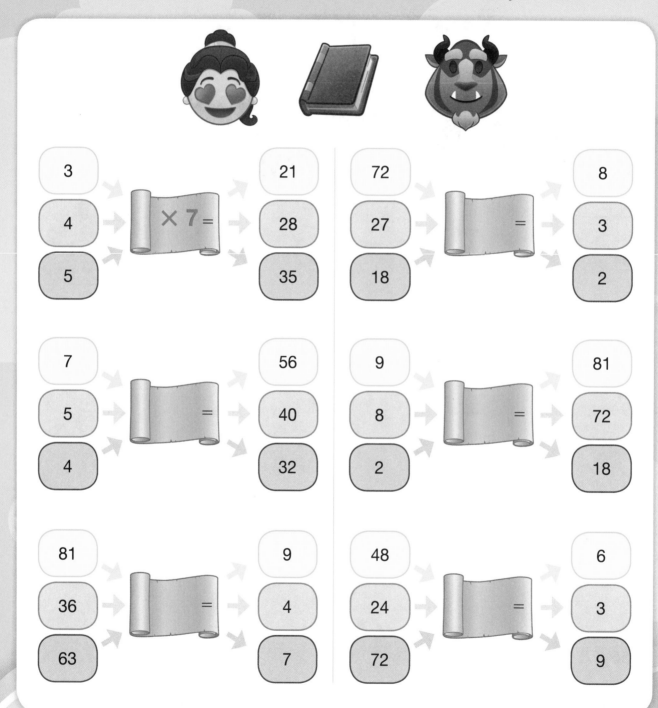

	× 7 =	
3		21
4		28
5		35

	=	
72		8
27		3
18		2

	=	
7		56
5		40
4		32

	=	
9		81
8		72
2		18

	=	
81		9
36		4
63		7

	=	
48		6
24		3
72		9

HINT Use either multiplication or division for each equation.

Fill In the Blanks

Maleficent is searching for Princess Aurora.
It's as if the princess has gone missing!

Determine the missing number in each equation.

$7 \times \underline{\hspace{2cm}} = 21$

$81 \div \underline{\hspace{2cm}} = 9$

$\underline{\hspace{2cm}} + 33 = 44$

$\underline{\hspace{2cm}} \div 9 = 8$

$10 \times \underline{\hspace{2cm}} = 110$

$110 + \underline{\hspace{2cm}} = 135$

$\underline{\hspace{2cm}} \div 4 = 12$

$5 \times \underline{\hspace{2cm}} = 75$

$\underline{\hspace{2cm}} - 66 = 11$

$152 - \underline{\hspace{2cm}} = 86$

$18 + \underline{\hspace{2cm}} = 70$

$\underline{\hspace{2cm}} \times 8 = 48$

$\underline{\hspace{2cm}} \div 10 = 8$

$52 - \underline{\hspace{2cm}} = 11$

$60 \div \underline{\hspace{2cm}} = 10$

$\underline{\hspace{2cm}} + 22 = 66$

HINT Use the opposite operation to help determine the missing number.

Fill In the Blanks

Watch out for Squirt! He is so fast. One minute he appears, and the next minute he is gone. It's just like multiplying by 1 and then 0.

Complete each multiplication sentence.

$11 \times 0 =$ _____

$11 \times 1 =$ _____

$26 \times 0 =$ _____

$26 \times 1 =$ _____

$108 \times 1 =$ _____

$90 \times 0 =$ _____

$145 \times 1 =$ _____

$200 \times 0 =$ _____

$486 \times 0 =$ _____

$225 \times 1 =$ _____

$425 \times 0 =$ _____

$1072 \times 1 =$ _____

$856 \times 0 =$ _____

$444 \times 1 =$ _____

$888 \times 0 =$ _____

$757 \times 1 =$ _____

HINT Look for the pattern when multiplying by 0 or 1. Use the pattern to finish the rest of the questions.

Fill In the Blanks

Woody and Buzz organize the toys into teams.
They could use a t-chart to plan how many toys are needed.

Complete the t-chart.

Number of Teams	Number of Toys
1	9
2	
3	
4	
5	
6	
7	
8	
9	
10	

How many toys are on 3 teams?

_____

How many toys are on 5 teams?

_____

How many toys are on 8 teams?

_____

What is the number pattern?

_____

_____

_____

GO TEAM

Puzzle Pieces

Rapunzel's hair grows a little bit every day.
She might want to keep track of how long it is.

Write the lengths in order from shortest to longest.

| 1 m | 98 cm | 25 cm | 400 mm |

_____ , _____ , _____ , _____

| 5 cm | 300 cm | 2 m | 55 mm |

_____ , _____ , _____ , _____

#HAIRGOALS

HINT Convert all the measurements to centimetres before putting them in order. Remember that 100 cm = 1 m and 10 mm = 1 cm.

Matching

Moana and Maui collect rainwater as they journey across the ocean.

How much water do they collect?

Match each measurement in millilitres to its equivalent in litres.

500 mL	5 L
1500 mL	0.1 L
250 mL	0.5 L
100 mL	2 L
5000 mL	1.5 L
2000 mL	3 L
2500 mL	0.9 L
900 mL	2.5 L
3000 mL	0.25 L

HINT Remember that 1000 mL = 1 L.

Picture Clues

Jack Skellington is loading up the sleigh with presents. Is there enough space?
Jack could determine the volume of the presents to see if they will fit.

Determine the volume of each present.
Each centimetre cube measures 1 cm x 1 cm x 1 cm.

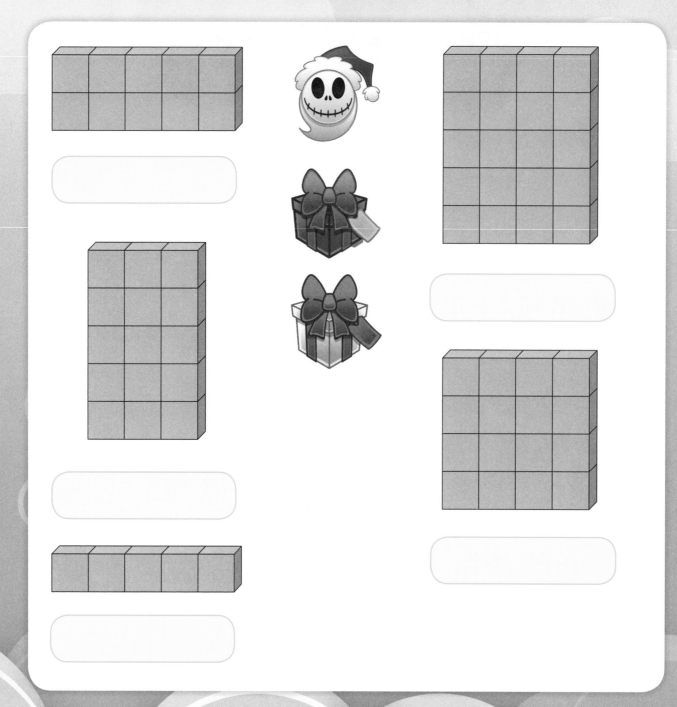

HINT Count the centimetre cubes to determine the volume of each present.

66

Fill In the Blanks

Mickey is giving presents to all his friends. He could estimate the length of each present to make sure they all fit in his car.

List five objects found in your home. Estimate their length.
Then measure each object.

Object	Estimate	Measurement

HINT Remember to include your unit of measurement, such as centimetres.

67

Picture Clues

Woody's arms are longer than Buzz's arms. But how much longer?
They could measure their arms to find out.

Use the ruler to measure the length of each object.

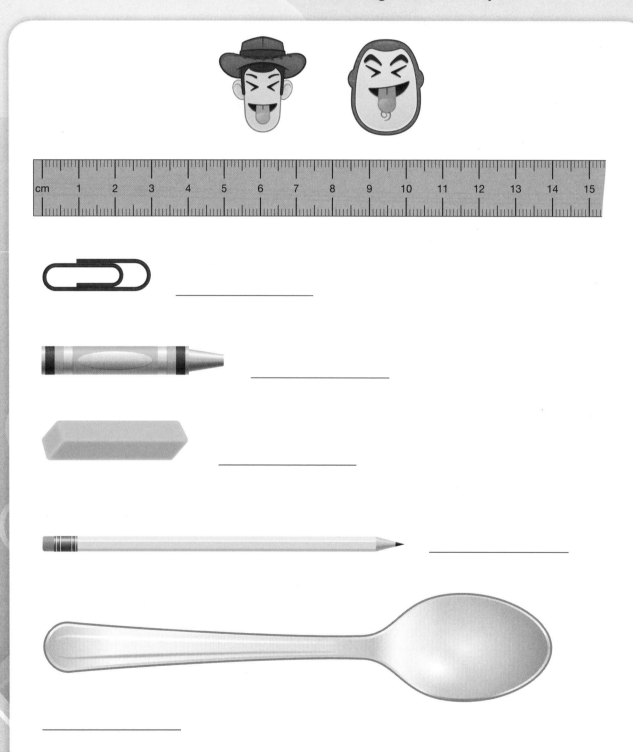

_____

_____

_____

_____

_____

68

Picture Clues

Aladdin wants to take Jasmine for a ride on the magic carpet.
He wants to choose the route with the greatest perimeter.

Determine the perimeter of each shape.
Each square on the grid represents 1 cm².

perimeter: _____

perimeter: _____

perimeter: _____

Which square or rectangle
has the greatest perimeter?

_____

_____

perimeter: _____

_____.

HINT To determine the perimeter of a square or
rectangle, add the length and width. Then multiply by 2.

69

Solve the Riddles

Mickey Mouse is building a doghouse for Pluto.
He needs to decide what length and width it should be.

Solve each riddle. Determine the missing dimensions.

1. A square has a perimeter of 16 cm.
   How long are each of its sides?

   _____

2. A rectangle has a perimeter of 24 cm. It has a length of 7 cm.
   What is its width?

   _____

3. A square has an area of 25 cm^2.
   How long is each side?

   _____

4. A rectangle has an area of 24 cm^2. It has a width of 4 cm.
   What is its length?

   _____

HINT To determine the area of a square
or rectangle, multiply the length by the width.

Fill In the Blanks

The White Rabbit has an appointment to see the Queen of Hearts. He looks at his watch and realizes that he is late!

Look at the White Rabbit's schedule. Draw the missing clock hands to show what time each event starts.

Leave home: 8:30 a.m.

First meeting with the Queen of Hearts: 9:15 a.m.

Eat lunch: 12:30 p.m.

Second meeting with the Queen of Hearts: 1:00 p.m.

Go home: 4:30 p.m.

HINT The short hand points to the hour.

Picture Clues

Donald Duck and Goofy want to do something together. They only have 80 minutes. What activity could they do?

The clocks show when each activity starts and finishes. Determine how long each activity is. Circle each activity that Goofy and Donald have time to do.

   The concert is

_____ minutes long.

   The cooking class is

_____ minutes long.

   Tobogganing is

_____ minutes long.

   The boat ride is

_____ minutes long.

HINT There are 60 minutes in 1 hour.

72

Matching

Simba looks at Pride Rock. The rocks form an angle.

Match each description to its angle.

less than right angle

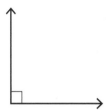

greater than right angle

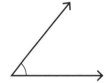

right angle

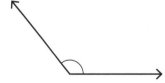

How could you describe the angle of Pride Rock?

_____

I'M GONNA RULE IT ALL

Picture Clues

Sulley gets ready to scare a child.
As he slowly opens the door, he creates an angle.

Write the angle shown on each protractor.

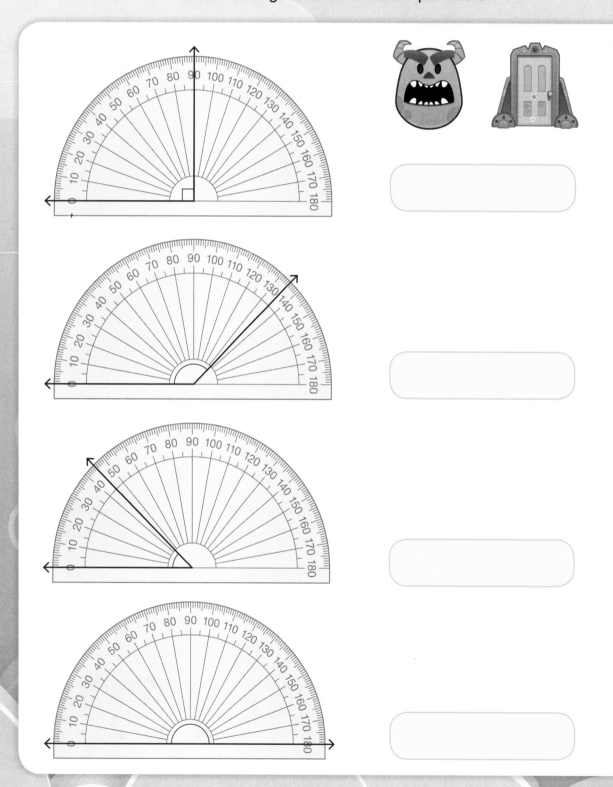

74

Picture Clues

As Simba walks across the plains, he sees many different shapes in the grasses and trees.

Complete the table. The first row is done for you.

Shape	Number of Sides of Equal Length	Number of Pairs of Parallel Sides	Number of Right Angles	Number of Lines of Symmetry
■	4	2	4	4
▬				
◆				
▰				
⬢				

75

Picture Clues

Mrs. Potts shows Chip a bowl of sugar cubes. A cube is a 3-D object.

Complete the table.

3-D Object	Name	Number of Edges	Number of Vertices	Number of Faces

HINT An **edge** is where two faces meet. A **vertex** (plural form: **vertices**) is where two or more edges meet.

Matching

The magic carpet is hiding from Aladdin. It hides by rolling up into a cylinder.
When it unrolls and lies flat, it is a rectangle.

Match each 3-D object to its net.

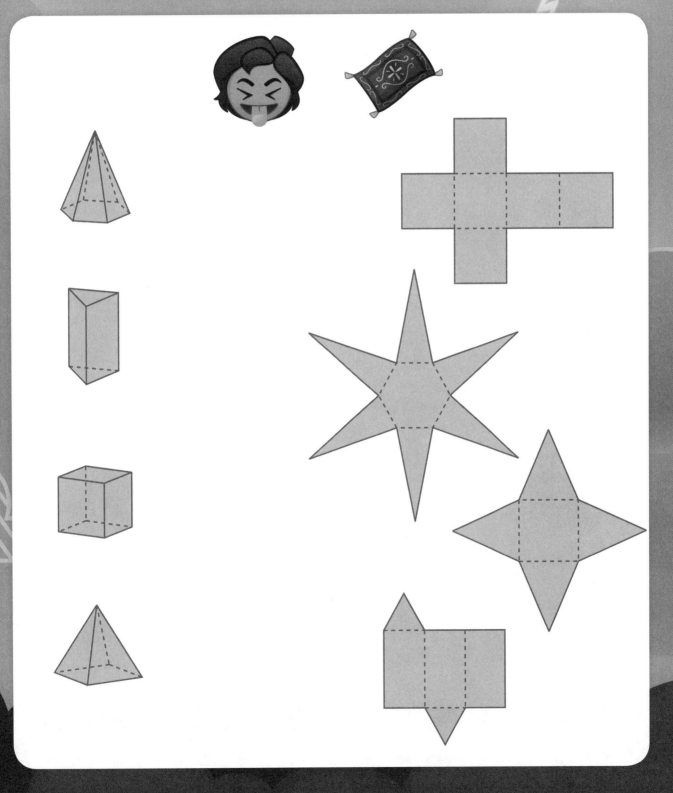

Fill In the Blanks

Alice is in Wonderland. The playing cards combine to form
3-D objects with edges, vertices, and faces.

Complete the table.

3-D Object	Name	Number of Edges	Number of Vertices	Number of Faces

HINT You can use the 3-D object flash cards on page 115 to help you.

Solve the Riddles

Scuttle thinks he knows a lot about human objects.
But he often doesn't have the right name for them!

Solve each riddle. Write the name of the 3-D object.

1. I have 12 edges and 6 triangle faces.

   What 3-D object am I?

   _____

2. I have an even number of edges and vertices.

   I have 6 rectangle faces.

   What 3-D object am I?

   _____

3. I have 8 vertices and 6 faces.

   What 3-D object am I?

   _____

Dinglehopper!

Colour to Complete

Wall-E finds an old fire extinguisher.
The fire extinguisher looks like a cylinder.

Match each prism. Then colour each blank prism to match the colour version.

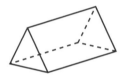

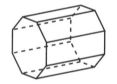

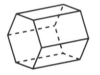

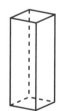

Word Search

Dory is looking everywhere for her parents.
She searches high and she searches low. She is on a fish search!

Complete the word search. Circle the name of each 3-D object.

HELP ME

R U LOST?

SPHERE

CUBE

CYLINDER

PRISM

CONE

PYRAMID

TETRAHEDRON

```
P  A  J  M  O  S  P  H  E  R  E
Y  D  O  C  W  K  O  A  S  D  N
R  E  L  Y  E  M  P  R  I  S  M
A  P  O  L  T  C  F  A  D  E  N
M  Q  U  I  N  U  Z  C  O  N  E
I  N  O  N  P  B  R  G  K  H  A
D  S  A  D  U  E  Y  E  S  U  D
T  E  S  E  K  A  D  M  W  A  L
T  E  T  R  A  H  E  D  R  O  N
G  W  X  L  O  N  R  A  W  M  M
```

Solve the Riddles

Ariel and Flounder are waiting to see King Triton. To pass the time, they could challenge each other with riddles to solve.

Solve each riddle to find the name of the 3-D objects.

Word Bank

triangle-based pyramid

pentagon-based prism

triangle-based prism

square-based pyramid

1. I have at least one square face.

   I have 5 faces altogether.

   What 3-D object am I?

   _____

2. I have 4 vertices and 6 edges.

   What 3-D object am I?

   _____

3. I have triangle and rectangle faces.

   I have 5 faces.

   What 3-D object am I?

   _____

4. I have a pentagon base.

   I have rectangular faces.

   What 3-D object am I?

   _____

HINT You can use the 3-D object flash cards on page 115 to help you.

Matching

Rapunzel sees lots of lanterns.
The lanterns are shaped like rectangle-based prisms.

Match each 3-D object with the correct number of vertices.

                    7 vertices

                    10 vertices

                    4 vertices

                    8 vertices

                    16 vertices

Picture Clues

The gang from Halloween Town may be scary,
but some them are also symmetrical.

Draw the line of symmetry for each face.

HINT An image is symmetrical when you can
draw a line through it and both halves are the same.

Colour to Complete

Maleficent is one of the most fearsome villains around! She has green skin and long horns. Her horns and face are symmetrical.

Colour each picture so that it is symmetrical.

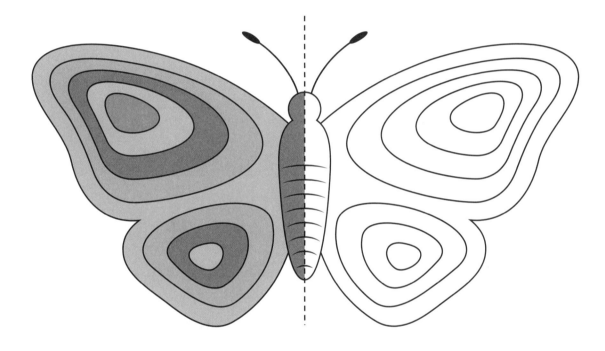

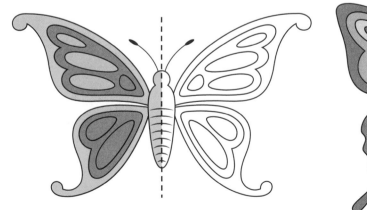
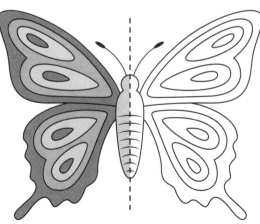

Maze

Dory is caught by the jellyfish!
Marlin needs to swim through the jellyfish to reach her.

Find a path through the maze.
Follow the shapes with two or more lines of symmetry.

Start

Finish

Picture Clues

Elsa creates snowflakes with her ice powers. Snowflakes are symmetrical.

Draw the lines of symmetry for each shape.
Write how many lines of symmetry there are.

HINT Trace each shape onto a piece of paper. Cut it out. Fold the paper in half several times. Check for the lines of symmetry.

Picture Clues

At Monsters, Inc., they do not scare children anymore. They make them laugh instead! Sulley looks in the mirror to practise making funny faces. His image is reflected.

Decide whether each image is a translation, rotation, or reflection.

 #FUNNY

  The image is a _____.

 The image is a _____.

 The image is a _____.

HINT Translation means "a slide." **Rotation** means "a turn." **Reflection** means "a flip."

Matching

Anna and Elsa are exploring the castle. They find a trunk.
They look inside. It's full of winter clothes.

Match each pair of images to the correct name for the transformation.

translation

reflection

rotation

Picture Clues

The toys are scattered across Andy's room.
Woody could create a map to show where each toy is located.

Use the map to answer each question.

WHERE ARE YOU?

What is in square B1?

_____

Start at D5. How could you get to the hockey stick?

_____

_____

In which square is the teddy bear?

_____

Start at the hockey stick. How could you get to the book?

_____

_____

How could you get from the toy box to the game controller?

_____

_____

 COME FIND ME!

Picture Clues

Donald Duck has a bag of marbles.
His marbles are all different colours.

Look at the bag of marbles. Use a word from the
Word Bank to describe each situation.

Word Bank

likely   unlikely   impossible   certain

What is the probability of selecting a marble
from this bag?

_____

What is the probability of selecting a blue marble?

_____

What is the probability of selecting a yellow marble?

_____

What is the probability of selecting a green marble?

_____

Picture Clues

Chief Bogo thinks it is unlikely that Judy will find the missing Mr. Otterton. Assistant Mayor Bellwether is certain that Judy can crack the case.

Look at the spinner. Use a word from the Word Bank to describe each situation.

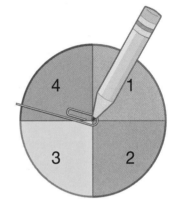

Word Bank

impossible   unlikely   equally likely

likely   certain

What is the probability that the spinner will stop on yellow?

_____

What is the probability that the spinner will stop on blue or yellow?

_____

What is the probability that the spinner will stop on a colour?

_____

What is the probability that the spinner will stop on red?

_____

What is the probability that the spinner will stop on brown?

_____

Colour to Complete

Genie grants nearly all wishes. There are only three wishes he cannot grant. It is likely that Aladdin's wishes will be granted.

Colour the gumballs to match each situation.

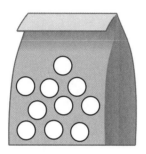

I am likely to pull out a purple gumball.

It is equally likely that I will pull out a yellow or green gumball.

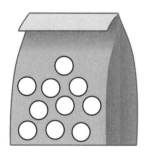

I will never pull out a blue gumball. I will always pull out a red gumball.

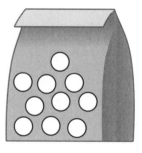

It is impossible that I will pull out a white gumball.

I am more likely to pull out an orange gumball. I am less likely to pull out a black gumball.

#POOF

Picture Clues

Judy works hard to land a job in Zootopia, the city of her dreams. She feels certain that working for the Zootopia Police Department will be everything she hoped for.

Look at the spinner. Use the probability words to describe each situation.

Word Bank

impossible   unlikely   likely   certain

What is the probability that the spinner will stop on the letter **R**?

_____

What is the probability that the spinner will stop on a letter?

_____

What is the probability that the spinner will stop on a vowel?

_____

What is the probability that the spinner will stop on a consonant?

_____

Graphing

Arendelle gets a lot of precipitation. In places that get a lot of precipitation, people record how much rain or snow falls.

Read the data shown in the tally chart.

What do you notice about the data in this tally chart?

_____

_____

Month	Precipitation in cm
January	卌 卌 卌 卌 卌 ||
February	卌 卌 卌 卌 |||
March	卌 卌 卌 卌
April	卌 卌 卌 卌
May	卌 卌 卌 卌 卌 卌 卌 卌
June	卌 卌 卌 卌 卌 卌 卌 卌 卌 ||||

Use the data in the tally chart to create a bar graph. Think about the title, headings, and labels. What interval will you use?

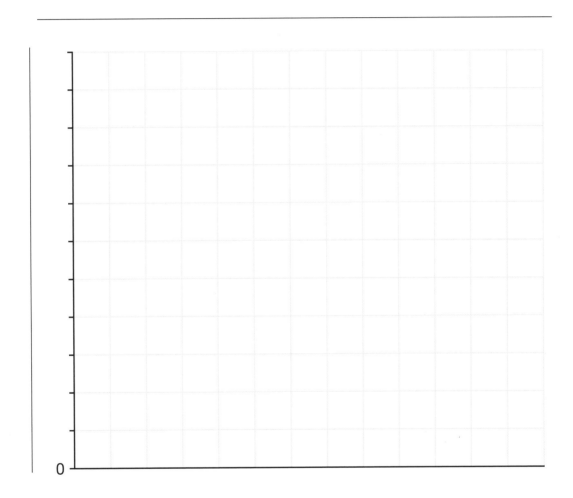

0

Fill In the Blanks

Mickey Mouse sees snowflakes everywhere!

What is the median number of snowflakes he sees?
Write each set of numbers in order. Then determine the median.

70 50 65 52 69

————, ————, ————, ————, ————

Median: _____

115 112 111 119 108 121 125

————, ————, ————, ————, ————, ————, ————

Median: _____

1025 1011 1276 1272 1188 1165 1347

————, ————, ————, ————, ————, ————, ————

Median: _____

HINT To find the median, first arrange the numbers from least to greatest. Then look for the number in the middle.

Matching

Alice is stuck in Wonderland. She wonders if everything that is happening is real or if she is in the middle of a dream.

Match each set of numbers to the correct median.

 HUH?

8 47 29 11 38 58 25   62

843 145 440 696 828   150

38 62 61 92 99 5 88   80

189 468 532 580 436 868   500

94 41 75 25 97 85   696

192 140 195 160 124 116   29

R U DREAMING?

HINT The **median** is the number in the middle of a set of numbers arranged from least to greatest. If there are two numbers in the middle, add them together and divide by two.

Answers

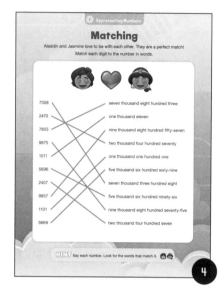

Representing Numbers
Matching
Aladdin and Jasmine love to be with each other. They are a perfect match!
Match each digit to the number in words.

7308	seven thousand eight hundred three
2470	one thousand eleven
7803	nine thousand eight hundred fifty-seven
9875	two thousand four hundred seventy
1011	one thousand one hundred one
5696	five thousand six hundred sixty-nine
2407	seven thousand three hundred eight
9857	five thousand six hundred ninety-six
1101	nine thousand eight hundred seventy-five
5669	two thousand four hundred seven

HINT Say each number. Look for the words that match it.

4

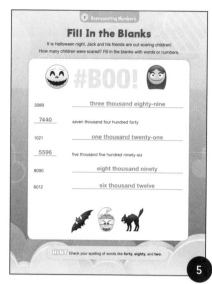

Representing Numbers
Fill In the Blanks
It is Halloween night. Jack and his friends are out scaring children!
How many children were scared? Fill in the blanks with words or numbers.

#BOO!

3089	three thousand eighty-nine
7440	seven thousand four hundred forty
1021	one thousand twenty-one
5596	five thousand five hundred ninety-six
8090	eight thousand ninety
6012	six thousand twelve

HINT Check your spelling of words like **forty**, **eighty**, and **two**.

5

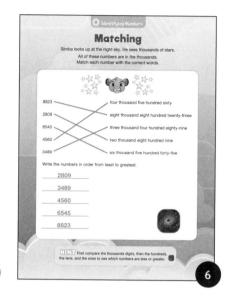

Identifying Numbers
Matching
Simba looks up at the night sky. He sees thousands of stars.
All of these numbers are in the thousands.
Match each number with the correct words.

8823	four thousand five hundred sixty
2809	eight thousand eight hundred twenty-three
6545	three thousand four hundred eighty-nine
4560	two thousand eight hundred nine
3489	six thousand five hundred forty-five

Write the numbers in order from least to greatest.

2809
3489
4560
6545
8823

HINT First compare the thousands digits, then the hundreds, the tens, and the ones to see which numbers are less or greater.

6

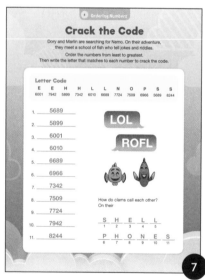

Ordering Numbers
Crack the Code
Dory and Marlin are searching for Nemo. On their adventure,
they meet a school of fish who tell jokes and riddles.
Order the numbers from least to greatest.
Then write the letter that matches each number to crack the code.

Letter Code

E	E	H	H	L	L	N	O	P	S	S
6001	7942	5899	7342	6010	6689	7724	7509	6966	5689	8244

1. 5689
2. 5899
3. 6001
4. 6010
5. 6689
6. 6966
7. 7342
8. 7509
9. 7724
10. 7942
11. 8244

LOL

ROFL

How do clams call each other?
On their

S	H	E	L	L
1	2	3	4	5

P	H	O	N	E	S
6	7	8	9	10	11

7

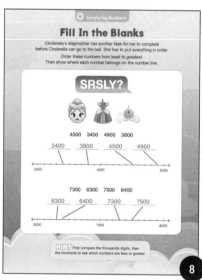

Comparing Numbers
Fill In the Blanks
Cinderella's stepmother has another task for her to complete
before Cinderella can go to the ball. She has to put everything in order.
Order these numbers from least to greatest.
Then show where each number belongs on the number line.

SRSLY?

4500 3400 4900 3800

3400   3800   4500   4900

3000   4000   5000

7300 6300 7500 6400

6300   6400   7300   7500

6000   7000   8000

HINT First compare the thousands digits, then the hundreds to see which numbers are less or greater.

8

Comparing Numbers
Fill In the Blanks
Beast is hungry! He wants to eat something right away.
Fill in the blanks with a less than < symbol or greater than > symbol.

4312	<	4321		1019	<	1020
6011	>	1106		3867	>	3786
5476	>	5467		2582	<	2825
9043	<	9403		6987	>	6879
2345	<	2534		1575	<	1757
8732	<	9732		2210	>	2201
7890	>	7809		5049	>	4950
5320	>	5302		7999	>	7888

HINT Think of < and > as the mouth of a hungry alligator. The mouth always opens to eat the greater number.

9

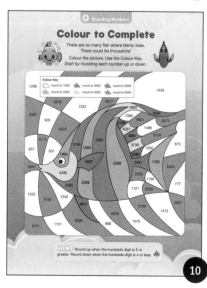

Rounding Numbers
Colour to Complete
There are so many fish where Nemo lives.
There could be thousands!
Colour the picture. Use the Colour Key.
Start by rounding each number up or down.

Colour Key
round to 1000 — round to 3000 — round to 5000
round to 2000 — round to 4000 — round to 6000

10

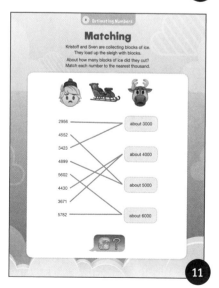

Estimating Numbers
Matching
Kristoff and Sven are collecting blocks of ice.
They load up the sleigh with blocks.
About how many blocks of ice did they cut?
Match each sleigh to the nearest thousand.

2956	about 3000
4552	
3423	about 4000
4899	
5602	about 5000
4430	
3671	about 6000
5782	

11

*Sample answers provided.

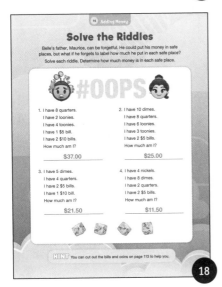

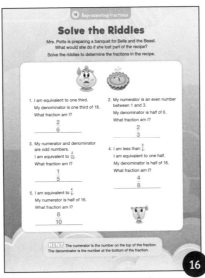

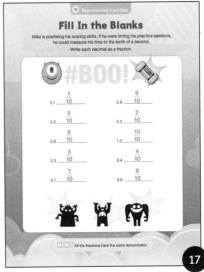

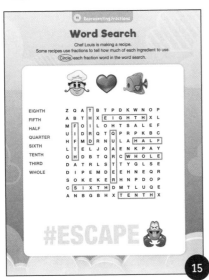

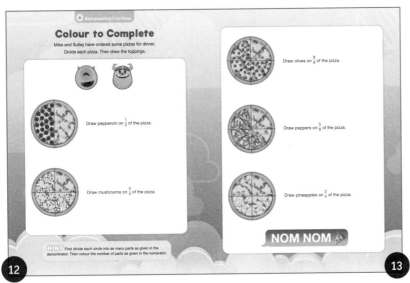

*Sample answers provided.

Answers

17 Adding and Subtracting Money

Solve the Riddles

Judy goes into the city to do some shopping.
Solve each riddle to determine how much money Judy has left
when she returns home.

1. Judy has 5 dimes, 4 quarters, 4 $5 bills, and 1 $10 bill.
How much money does she have?

Judy has $31.50.

Judy buys some carrots for dinner.
The carrots cost $12.50.
How much money does she have left?

Judy has $19.00 left.

2. Judy has 16 quarters and 3 $5 bills.
How much money does she have?

Judy has $19.00.

Judy spends $11 on a gift for her parents.
How much money does she have left?

Judy has $8.00 left.

3. Judy has 12 quarters and 1 $5 bill.
How much money does she have?

Judy has $8.00.

Judy buys a new book that costs $7.95.
How much money does she have left?

Judy has $0.05 left.

HINT First add the total amount of money Judy has to spend.
Then subtract each item to determine how much she has left.

21

18 Adding Using Mental Math

Fill In the Blanks

Ariel has many treasures in her secret grotto.
She keeps track of them all in her mind.
Use mental math strategies to determine each sum.

26 + 52 = 78	74 + 25 = 99
41 + 45 = 86	57 + 90 = 147
38 + 29 = 67	51 + 44 = 95
63 + 18 = 81	21 + 53 = 74
19 + 29 = 48	61 + 15 = 76
17 + 57 = 74	65 + 50 = 115
44 + 52 = 96	41 + 37 = 78
28 + 33 = 61	73 + 16 = 89

AWESOME!

HINT You can use the 100-chart on page 111 to help you.

22

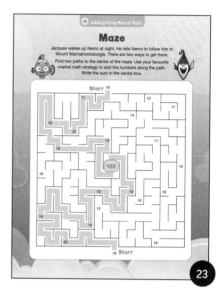

19 Adding Using Mental Math

Maze

Jacques wakes up Nemo at night. He tells Nemo to follow him to
Mount Wannahockaloogie. There are two ways to get there.
Find two paths to the centre of the maze. Use your favourite
mental math strategy to add the numbers along the path.
Write the sum in the centre box.

Start 18

100

Start

23

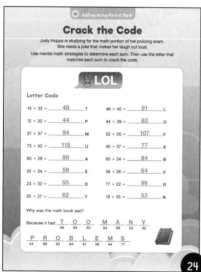

20 Adding Using Mental Math

Crack the Code

Judy Hopps is studying for the math portion of her policing exam.
She reads a joke that makes her laugh out loud.
Use mental math strategies to determine each sum. Then use the letter that
matches each sum to crack the code.

LOL

Letter Code

15 + 33 = 48	T	46 + 45 = 91	L
12 + 32 = 44	P	44 + 39 = 83	O
37 + 57 = 94	M	52 + 55 = 107	F
73 + 42 = 115	U	40 + 37 = 77	S
60 + 28 = 88	A	60 + 24 = 84	B
25 + 34 = 59	E	38 + 26 = 64	V
23 + 32 = 55	D	77 + 22 = 99	R
25 + 37 = 62		18 + 35 = 53	

Why was the math book sad?

Because it had T O O M A N Y
48 83 83 94 88 53 62

P R O B L E M S
44 99 83 84 91 59 94 77

24

21 Subtracting Using Mental Math

Maze

The Beast has to find true love before the rose loses all its petals.
Find two paths to the centre of the maze.
Use mental math to subtract the numbers along each path.
Write the difference in the centre box.

Start 100

6

Start

25

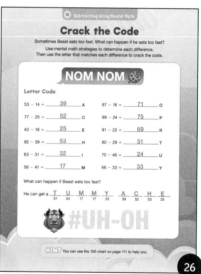

22 Subtracting Using Mental Math

Crack the Code

Sometimes Beast eats too fast. What can happen if he eats too fast?
Use mental math strategies to determine each difference.
Then use the letter that matches each difference to crack the code.

NOM NOM

Letter Code

53 − 14 = 39	A	87 − 16 = 71	O
77 − 25 = 52	C	99 − 24 = 75	P
43 − 18 = 25	E	91 − 22 = 69	R
92 − 39 = 53	H	80 − 29 = 51	T
63 − 31 = 32	I	70 − 46 = 24	U
58 − 41 = 17	Y	66 − 33 = 33	Y

What can happen if Beast eats too fast?

He can get a T U M M Y A C H E
51 24 17 17 33 39 52 53 25

#UH-OH

HINT You can use the 100-chart on page 111 to help you.

26

23 Subtracting Using Mental Math

Fill In the Blanks

Andy is moving. As the moving boxes are packed up, they are taken away.
It's hard for Woody to keep track of how many boxes there are!
Use mental math strategies to determine each difference.

98 − 27 = 71	58 − 41 = 17
71 − 19 = 52	50 − 17 = 33
64 − 27 = 37	27 − 11 = 16
83 − 62 = 21	28 − 13 = 15
31 − 17 = 14	43 − 20 = 23
45 − 32 = 13	52 − 16 = 36
93 − 62 = 31	65 − 50 = 15
85 − 33 = 52	44 − 13 = 31

27

24 Adding 4-Digit Numbers

Crack the Code

Marlin and Dory know that friends are important.
Friends stick with you through thick and thin!
Determine each sum. Then use the letter that matches
each sum to crack the code.

Letter Code

1128	3479	6350	3468
+ 6534	+ 5521	+ 2260	+ 5486
7662 C	9000 T	8610 H	8954 E

1107	8348	1557	4932
+ 1578	+ 1607	+ 1884	+ 4015
2685 O	9955 M	3441 N	8947 U

Why do number lines make good friends?

Because you can always C O U N T
7662 9000 8947 3441 9000

O N T H E M
2685 3441 9000 8610 8954 9955

BFF

HINT You can use the place value chart on page 112 to help you.

28

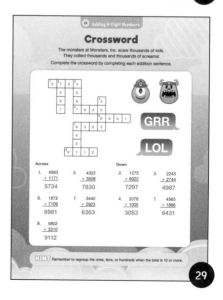

25 Adding 4-Digit Numbers

Crossword

The monsters at Monsters, Inc. scare thousands of kids.
They collect thousands and thousands of screams!
Complete the crossword by completing each addition sentence.

GRR

LOL

Across

1. 4563	5. 4322
+ 1171	+ 3508
5734	7830

6. 1872	7. 3440
+ 7109	+ 2923
8981	6363

8. 5802	
+ 3310	
9112	

Down

2. 1275	3. 2243
+ 6022	+ 2744
7297	4987

4. 2078	4. 4565
+ 1005	+ 1866
3083	6431

HINT Remember to regroup the ones, tens, or hundreds when the total is 10 or more.

29

---

* Sample answers provided.

Puzzle Pieces

Elsa creates thousands of snowflakes that cover the castle.
How many snowflakes does she create in total?
Use the puzzle pieces to complete each addition sentence.
Write the numbers in the answer boxes.

1.

| 4232 | 3145 | 2505 | 5480 |

2505 + 3145 = 5650   4232 + 5480 = 9712

2.

| 4595 | 1593 | 2059 | 6776 |

1593 + 6776 = 8369   2059 + 4595 = 6654

HINT Try different combinations of numbers to determine the total.

30

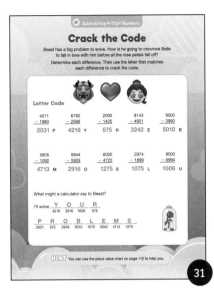

Crack the Code

Beast has a big problem to solve. How is he going to convince Belle to fall in love with him before all the rose petals fall off?
Determine each difference. Then use the letter that matches each difference to crack the code.

Letter Code

4011	6782	2000	8143	9000
− 1980	− 2566	− 1425	− 4901	− 3990
2031 P	4216 Y	575 R	3242 E	5010 B

5805	8844	6000	2974	8000
− 1092	− 5928	− 4725	− 1899	− 6994
4713 M	2916 O	1275 S	1075 L	1006 U

What might a calculator say to Beast?

I'll solve Y O U R
       4216 2916 1006 575

P R O B L E M S
2031 575 2916 5010 1075 3242 4713 1275

31

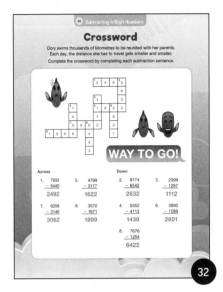

Crossword

Dory swims thousands of kilometres to be reunited with her parents.
Each day, the distance she has to travel gets smaller and smaller.
Complete the crossword by completing each subtraction sentence.

WAY TO GO!

Across

1. 7932   5. 4799
  − 5440   − 3177
  2492   1622

7. 6208   9. 3570
  − 3146   − 1671
  3062   1899

Down

2. 9174   3. 2399
  − 6542   − 1287
  2632   1112

4. 5552   6. 3890
  − 4113   − 1089
  1439   2801

8. 7676
  − 1254
  6422

32

Fill In the Blanks

Mickey Mouse the Magician is trying some new magic.
He can make things disappear and reappear.
Some of the numbers have disappeared! Determine the missing number for each subtraction sentence.

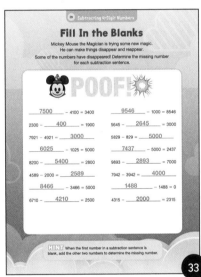

POOF!

7500 − 4100 = 3400   9546 − 1000 = 8546

2300 − 400 = 1900   5645 − 2645 = 3000

7921 − 4921 = 3000   5829 − 829 = 5000

6025 − 1025 = 5000   7437 − 5000 = 2437

8200 − 5400 = 2800   9893 − 2893 = 7000

4589 − 2000 = 2589   7942 − 3942 = 4000

8466 − 3466 = 5000   1488 − 1488 = 0

6710 − 4210 = 2500   4315 − 2000 = 2315

HINT When the first number in a subtraction sentence is blank, add the other two numbers to determine the missing number.

33

Function Box

Some of the doors lead to rooms that have more than one child inside.
The monsters can collect two or three or more screams per door!
If Mike enters 3 doors and collects the same number of screams each time, how many screams were collected at each door if the total is 12?

3 doors × 4 screams = 12 screams
Determine the missing number for each multiplication sentence.

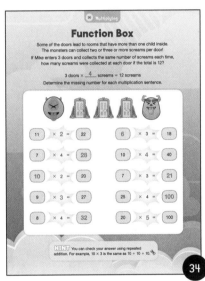

11 × 2 = 22   6 × 3 = 18

7 × 4 = 28   10 × 4 = 40

10 × 2 = 20   7 × 3 = 21

9 × 3 = 27   25 × 4 = 100

8 × 4 = 32   20 × 5 = 100

HINT You can check your answer using repeated addition. For example, 10 × 3 is the same as 10 + 10 + 10.

34

Crack the Code

Cinderella does everything for her stepsisters. She might even have to do her stepsisters' math homework!
Determine each product. Then use the letter that matches each product to crack the code.

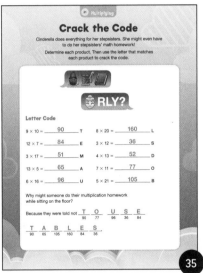

RLY?

Letter Code

9 × 10 = 90 T   8 × 20 = 160 L

12 × 7 = 84 E   3 × 12 = 36 S

3 × 17 = 51 M   4 × 13 = 52 D

13 × 5 = 65 A   7 × 11 = 77 O

6 × 16 = 96 U   5 × 21 = 105 Y

Why might someone do their multiplication homework while sitting on the floor?

Because they were told not T O   U S E
                        90 77 96 36 84

T A B L E S
90 65 105 160 84 36

35

Function Box

Chief Bogo tells Judy to write 100 parking tickets. Judy is going to do even better than that! She will write two times as many parking tickets before noon!
Determine the missing number for each multiplication sentence.

#GOALS

4 × 8 = 32   9 × 6 = 54

8 × 7 = 56   7 × 8 = 56

3 × 8 = 24   9 × 8 = 72

4 × 7 = 28   5 × 8 = 40

5 × 7 = 35   3 × 7 = 21

HINT You can use the multiplication chart on page 112 to help you.

36

Fill In the Blanks

Aladdin and Jasmine are looking at the apples at the market.
The apples are arranged in rows of equal length. They could use multiplication to determine the total number.
Determine each product.

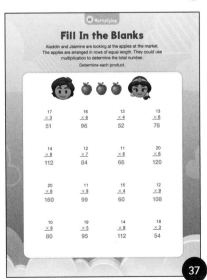

17	16	13	13
×3	×6	×4	×6
51	96	52	78

14	12	11	20
×8	×7	×6	×6
112	84	66	120

20	11	15	12
×8	×9	×4	×9
160	99	60	108

10	19	14	18
×8	×5	×8	×3
80	95	112	54

37

Crack the Code

Goofy just saw someone eat their homework!
Why would anyone eat their homework?
Complete each division sentence.
Then use the letter that matches each quotient to crack the code.

YUMMY!

Letter Code

12 ÷ 3 = 4 O   35 ÷ 5 = 7 K

8 ÷ 4 = 2 I   8 ÷ 8 = 1 T

30 ÷ 6 = 5 E   18 ÷ 6 = 3 F

27 ÷ 3 = 9 N   64 ÷ 8 = 8 A

24 ÷ 4 = 6 P   7 ÷ 7 = 1 L

Why would anyone eat their homework?

Because the teacher said it was a P I E C E
                              6 2 5 9 5

O F   C A K E
4 3 9 8 7 5

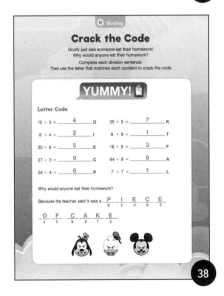

38

* Sample answers provided.

Answers

Function Box

The Little Green Aliens are going on a mission.
They divide themselves into groups.
Determine the missing number for each division sentence.

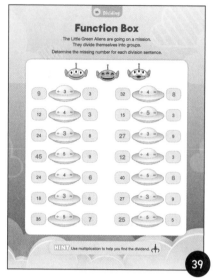

9 ÷ 3 =	**3**		32 ÷ 4 =	**8**	
12 ÷ 4 =	**3**		15 ÷ 5 =	**3**	
24 ÷ 3 =	**8**		27 ÷ 3 =	**9**	
45 ÷ 5 =	**9**		12 ÷ 4 =	**3**	
24 ÷ 4 =	**6**		40 ÷ 5 =	**8**	
18 ÷ 3 =	**6**		27 ÷ 3 =	**9**	
35 ÷ 5 =	**7**		25 ÷ 5 =	**5**	

HINT Use multiplication to help you find the dividend.

39

Fill In the Blanks

Rapunzel loves looking at the lanterns in the sky.
She could use division to divide them evenly into groups.
Complete each division sentence.

63 ÷ 3 =	**21**	70 ÷ 5 =	**14**
52 ÷ 4 =	**13**	66 ÷ 2 =	**33**
44 ÷ 2 =	**22**	72 ÷ 6 =	**12**
75 ÷ 5 =	**15**	56 ÷ 4 =	**14**
66 ÷ 6 =	**11**	60 ÷ 3 =	**20**
36 ÷ 2 =	**18**	60 ÷ 5 =	**12**
80 ÷ 5 =	**16**	48 ÷ 2 =	**24**
90 ÷ 2 =	**45**	90 ÷ 5 =	**18**
65 ÷ 5 =	**13**	100 ÷ 2 =	**50**

GO LIVE YOUR DREAM!

HINT Multiply the quotient by the divisor to check your answer.

40

Function Box

While collecting garbage on Earth, Wall-E finds an old calculator.
He presses the buttons.
What numbers appear on the calculator? Determine the missing
number for each division sentence.

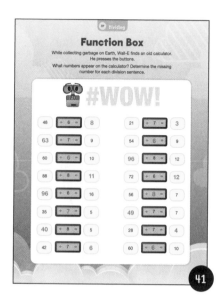

#WOW!

48	÷ 6 =	8	21	÷ 7 =	3
63	÷ 7 =	9	54	÷ 6 =	9
60	÷ 6 =	10	96	÷ 8 =	12
88	÷ 8 =	11	72	÷ 6 =	12
96	÷ 6 =	16	56	÷ 8 =	7
35	÷ 7 =	5	49	÷ 7 =	7
40	÷ 8 =	5	28	÷ 7 =	4
42	÷ 7 =	6	60	÷ 6 =	10

41

Picture Clues

Daisy Duck picks tulips from her garden.
She divides them into bunches.

#SPRING

Count the number of tulips. **33**

How many groups of 5 tulips are there? **6**

How many tulips are left over? **3**

Write the division sentence. **33 ÷ 5 = 6, remainder 3**

HINT Circle groups of 5 tulips. How many
groups are there? How many tulips are left over?

42

Matching

Goofy is dividing everyone into soccer teams.
He wants the teams to be even so that no one is left out.
Determine how many people can be divided into how many teams.
Match each division statement to the remainders.

36 ÷ 8 — remainder 1
44 ÷ 7 — remainder 2
25 ÷ 9 — remainder 3
30 ÷ 3 — remainder 4
15 ÷ 2 — remainder 5
23 ÷ 5 — remainder 6
20 ÷ 7 — remainder 7
50 ÷ 8 — no remainder

FRIENDS 4EVER!

43

Fill In the Blanks

Moana and the islanders are collecting coconuts.
About how many coconuts do they collect?
Estimate each sum. Round each number first. Then add to estimate the sum.

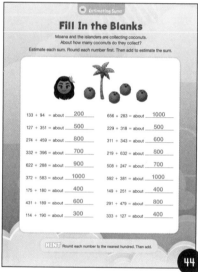

133 + 94 = about	**200**	656 + 283 = about	**1000**
127 + 351 = about	**500**	229 + 318 = about	**500**
274 + 459 = about	**800**	311 + 343 = about	**600**
332 + 396 = about	**700**	219 + 632 = about	**800**
622 + 288 = about	**900**	508 + 247 = about	**700**
372 + 583 = about	**1000**	592 + 381 = about	**1000**
175 + 180 = about	**400**	149 + 251 = about	**400**
431 + 189 = about	**600**	291 + 479 = about	**800**
114 + 190 = about	**300**	333 + 127 = about	**400**

HINT Round each number to the nearest hundred. Then add.

44

Fill In the Blanks

Sulley looks for Boo's door. But there are hundreds of doors in the factory!
The doors get taken away by the hanging conveyor belts.
About how many doors are taken away? Estimate each difference. Round each
number first. Then subtract to estimate the difference.

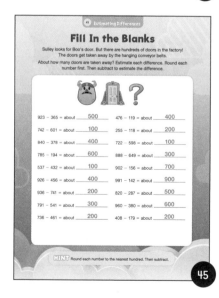

923 − 365 = about	**500**	476 − 119 = about	**400**
742 − 601 = about	**100**	255 − 118 = about	**200**
840 − 378 = about	**400**	722 − 598 = about	**100**
785 − 194 = about	**600**	888 − 649 = about	**300**
537 − 432 = about	**100**	902 − 156 = about	**700**
926 − 456 = about	**400**	991 − 142 = about	**900**
936 − 741 = about	**200**	820 − 287 = about	**500**
791 − 541 = about	**300**	960 − 380 = about	**600**
736 − 461 = about	**200**	408 − 179 = about	**200**

HINT Round each number to the nearest hundred. Then subtract.

45

Matching

Simba sees herds of different animals on the grasslands.
Each herd can have hundreds of animals.
About how many animals are there? Match each number in the
addition statement to the best estimate. The first one is done for you.

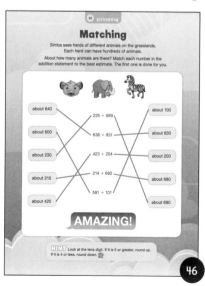

about 640 — 225 + 689 — about 100
about 600 — 636 + 831 — about 830
about 230 — 423 + 204 — about 200
about 210 — 214 + 682 — about 680
about 420 — 591 + 101 — about 690

AMAZING!

HINT Look at the tens digit. If it is 5 or greater, round up.
If it is 4 or less, round down.

46

Fill In the Blanks

Genie uses magic to change objects from one thing to another.
You can use multiplication to change numbers.
Determine the product for each multiplication sentence.

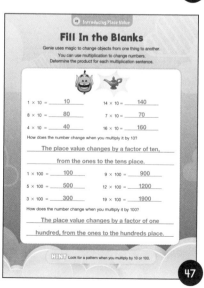

1 × 10 =	**10**	14 × 10 =	**140**
8 × 10 =	**80**	7 × 10 =	**70**
4 × 10 =	**40**	16 × 10 =	**160**

How does the number change when you multiply it by 10?

The place value changes by a factor of ten,
from the ones to the tens place.

1 × 100 =	**100**	9 × 100 =	**900**
5 × 100 =	**500**	12 × 100 =	**1200**
3 × 100 =	**300**	19 × 100 =	**1900**

How does the number change when you multiply it by 100?

The place value changes by a factor of one
hundred, from the ones to the hundreds place.

HINT Look for a pattern when you multiply by 10 or 100.

47

104

Sample answers provided.

Fill In the Blanks

Elsa does not want anyone to know about her ice powers. She's worried that thousands of people will find out at her coronation!
Fill in the blanks to show each number in its expanded form.

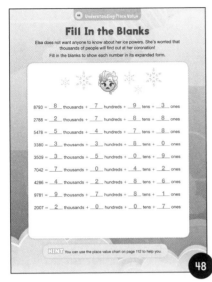

8793 = __8__ thousands + __7__ hundreds + __9__ tens + __3__ ones

2788 = __2__ thousands + __7__ hundreds + __8__ tens + __8__ ones

5478 = __5__ thousands + __4__ hundreds + __7__ tens + __8__ ones

3380 = __3__ thousands + __3__ hundreds + __8__ tens + __0__ ones

3509 = __3__ thousands + __5__ hundreds + __0__ tens + __9__ ones

7042 = __7__ thousands + __0__ hundreds + __4__ tens + __2__ ones

4286 = __4__ thousands + __2__ hundreds + __8__ tens + __6__ ones

9781 = __9__ thousands + __7__ hundreds + __8__ tens + __1__ ones

2007 = __2__ thousands + __0__ hundreds + __0__ tens + __7__ ones

HINT You can use the place value chart on page 112 to help you.

48

Matching

Mike and Sulley are in trouble. After Boo follows them into their world, their problems expand and get bigger and bigger!
Match each number to its expanded form.

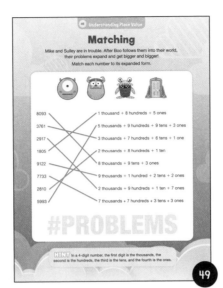

8093 — 1 thousand + 8 hundreds + 5 ones

3761 — 5 thousands + 9 hundreds + 9 tens + 3 ones

2917 — 3 thousands + 7 hundreds + 6 tens + 1 one

1805 — 2 thousands + 8 hundreds + 1 ten

9122 — 8 thousands + 9 tens + 3 ones

7733 — 9 thousands + 1 hundred + 2 tens + 2 ones

2810 — 2 thousands + 9 hundreds + 1 ten + 7 ones

5993 — 7 thousands + 7 hundreds + 3 tens + 3 ones

#PROBLEMS

HINT In a 4-digit number, the first digit is the thousands, the second is the hundreds, the third is the tens, and the fourth is the ones.

49

Picture Clues

Moana and Pua go down to the beach.
While Moana looks out at the ocean, Pua sits in the shade.
Count the shaded parts of each picture. Determine the decimal value.

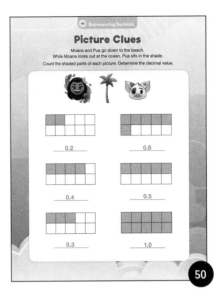

0.2   0.6

0.4   0.5

0.3   1.0

50

Puzzle Pieces

Cinderella has to put everything in order before she goes to bed.
Write these decimals in order from least to greatest.

0.7   0.3   0.1   0.5

__0.1__ , __0.3__ , __0.5__ , __0.7__

0.6   0.8   0.4   0.2

__0.2__ , __0.4__ , __0.6__ , __0.8__

HINT The smaller the tenths digit, the smaller the decimal.

51

Maze

Jafar wants to be the greatest!
He will do whatever it takes to be the greatest.
Find your way through the maze.
Follow the numbers from least to greatest.

Start

Finish

HINT Compare the tenths and then the hundredths digits to see which decimal is the greatest.

52

Crack the Code

Mickey told Minnie that he has a present for her.
But now he can't find it! He is nervous.
Write each fraction as a decimal.
Then write the letter that matches each decimal to crack the code.

THANK U!

Letter Code

A	E	H	N	O	S	T	W
$\frac{3}{5}$	$\frac{4}{10}$	$\frac{1}{10}$	$\frac{7}{10}$	$\frac{1}{5}$	$\frac{9}{10}$	$\frac{4}{5}$	$\frac{1}{2}$
0.6	0.4	0.1	0.7	0.2	0.9	0.8	0.5

Why couldn't the fraction relax?

It __W__ __A__ __S__ __T__ __W__ __O__
   0.5 0.6 0.9 0.8 0.5 0.2

__T__ __E__ __N__ __T__ __H__ __S__
0.8 0.4 0.7 0.8 0.1 0.9

53

Matching

Marlin and Dory are racing through the jellyfish. They are competing to see who is fastest. They could measure their time to the nearest tenth of a second.
Match each decimal to the correct fraction.

0.1 — five tenths
0.7 — nine tenths
0.4 — six tenths
0.5 — three tenths
0.6 — seven tenths
0.2 — eight tenths
0.8 — four tenths
0.3 — one tenth
0.9 — two tenths

EAT MY BUBBLES!

HINT Say each decimal to hear the words.

54

Fill In the Blanks

Mickey and Minnie are baking together.
They have to convert the fractions in the recipe to decimals.
Write each fraction as a decimal.

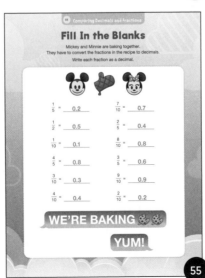

$\frac{1}{5}$ = __0.2__ $\frac{7}{10}$ = __0.7__

$\frac{1}{2}$ = __0.5__ $\frac{2}{5}$ = __0.4__

$\frac{1}{10}$ = __0.1__ $\frac{8}{10}$ = __0.8__

$\frac{4}{5}$ = __0.8__ $\frac{3}{5}$ = __0.6__

$\frac{3}{10}$ = __0.3__ $\frac{9}{10}$ = __0.9__

$\frac{4}{10}$ = __0.4__ $\frac{2}{10}$ = __0.2__

WE'RE BAKING

YUM!

55

Fill In the Blanks

Mike likes his day to follow the same pattern: get up, go to work, scare some children, go home.
Write the next 3 numbers in each number pattern.
Then write the pattern rule. The first one is done for you.

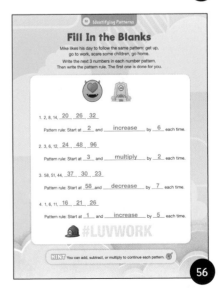

1. 2, 8, 14, __20__ __26__ __32__
Pattern rule: Start at __2__ and __increase__ by __6__ each time.

2. 3, 6, 12, __24__ __48__ __96__
Pattern rule: Start at __3__ and __multiply__ by __2__ each time.

3. 58, 51, 44, __37__ __30__ __23__
Pattern rule: Start at __58__ and __decrease__ by __7__ each time.

4. 1, 6, 11, __16__ __21__ __26__
Pattern rule: Start at __1__ and __increase__ by __5__ each time.

#LUVWORK

HINT You can add, subtract, or multiply to continue each pattern.

56

---

*Sample answers provided.

Answers

Page 57 — Identifying Patterns

Fill In the Blanks

Mickey is trying to get his magic spell right. More brooms appear, all carrying buckets of water! Write the pattern rule for each number pattern.

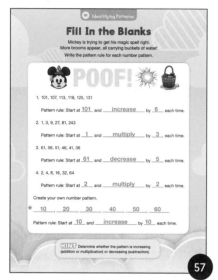

POOF!

1. 101, 107, 113, 119, 125, 131
   Pattern rule: Start at **101** and **increase** by **6** each time.

2. 1, 3, 9, 27, 81, 243
   Pattern rule: Start at **1** and **multiply** by **3** each time.

3. 61, 56, 51, 46, 41, 36
   Pattern rule: Start at **61** and **decrease** by **5** each time.

4. 2, 4, 8, 16, 32, 64
   Pattern rule: Start at **2** and **multiply** by **2** each time.

Create your own number pattern.

* **10** **20** **30** **40** **50** **60**

Pattern rule: Start at **10** and **increase** by **10** each time.

HINT Determine whether the pattern is increasing (addition or multiplication) or decreasing (subtraction).

57

Page 58 — Balancing Equations

Matching

Kristoff and Sven are loading the sleigh. All the packages must be balanced, or else they'll fall off! Equations must be balanced, too! Match the equations so they are balanced.

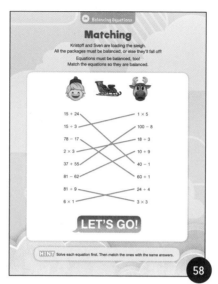

15 + 24 — 1 × 5
15 + 3 — 100 − 8
78 − 17 — 18 ÷ 3
2 × 3 — 10 + 9
37 ÷ 55 — 40 − 1
81 − 62 — 60 + 1
81 ÷ 9 — 24 + 4
6 × 1 — 3 × 3

LET'S GO!

HINT Solve each equation first. Then match the ones with the same answers.

58

Page 59 — Balancing Equations

Fill In the Blanks

Moana tries to balance four coconuts in her arms without any of them falling. Can you keep four numbers balanced? Fill in the blanks to complete each equation. Both sides of the equation have to balance. Space is provided for you to show your work.

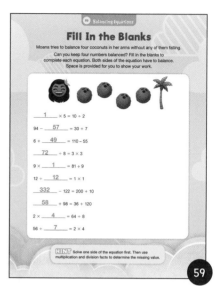

1 × 5 = 10 ÷ 2

94 − **57** = 30 + 7

6 + **49** = 110 − 55

72 ÷ 8 = 3 × 2

9 × **1** = 81 ÷ 9

12 ÷ **12** = 1 × 1

332 − 122 = 200 + 10

58 + 98 = 36 + 120

2 × **4** = 64 ÷ 8

56 ÷ **7** = 2 × 4

HINT Solve one side of the equation first. Then use multiplication and division facts to determine the missing value.

59

Page 60 — Missing Numbers

Function Box

Belle loves books. The bookstore in town does not have many books. The Beast has lots of books. Complete each equation. The first one is done for you.

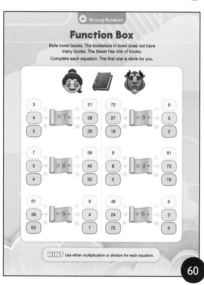

3
4 → ×7 → 28
5 → 35

21
27 → ÷9 → 3
18 → 2

72 → 8

7
5 → ×8 → 40
4 → 32

56
9 → ×9 → 72
8 → 2
18

81
36 → ÷9 → 4
63 → 7

9
48 → ÷8 → 6
24 → 3
72 → 9

HINT Use either multiplication or division for each equation.

60

Page 61 — Determining Missing Numbers

Fill In the Blanks

Maleficent is searching for Princess Aurora. It's as if the princess has gone missing! Determine the missing number in each equation.

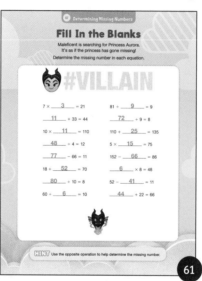

#VILLAIN

7 × **3** = 21
11 + 33 = 44
10 × **11** = 110
48 ÷ 4 = 12
77 − 66 = 11
18 + **52** = 70
80 ÷ 10 = 8
60 ÷ **6** = 10

81 + **9** = 9
72 ÷ 9 = 8
110 + **25** = 135
5 × **15** = 75
152 − **66** = 86
6 × 8 = 48
52 − **41** = 11
44 + 22 = 66

HINT Use the opposite operation to help determine the missing number.

61

Page 62 — Multiplying by 0 and 1

Fill In the Blanks

Watch out for Squirt! He is so fast. One minute he appears, and the next minute he is gone. It's just like multiplying by 1 and then 0. Complete each multiplication sentence.

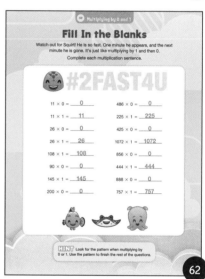

#2FAST4U

11 × 0 = **0**
11 × 1 = **11**
26 × 0 = **0**
26 × 1 = **26**
108 × 1 = **108**
90 × 0 = **0**
145 × 1 = **145**
200 × 0 = **0**

486 × 0 = **0**
225 × 1 = **225**
425 × 0 = **0**
1072 × 1 = **1072**
856 × 0 = **0**
444 × 1 = **444**
888 × 0 = **0**
757 × 1 = **757**

HINT Look for the pattern when multiplying by 0 or 1. Use the pattern to finish the rest of the questions.

62

Page 63 — Determining Patterns

Fill In the Blanks

Woody and Buzz organize the toys into teams. They could use a t-chart to plan how many toys are needed. Complete the t-chart.

Number of Teams	Number of Toys
1	9
2	18
3	27
4	36
5	45
6	54
7	63
8	72
9	81
10	90

How many toys are on 3 teams?
27 toys are on 3 teams.

How many toys are on 5 teams?
45 toys are on 5 teams.

How many toys are on 8 teams?
72 toys are on 8 teams.

What is the number pattern?
Multiply the term by 9 or add 9 each time.

GO TEAM

63

Page 64 — Ordering Length

Puzzle Pieces

Rapunzel's hair grows a little bit every day. She might want to keep track of how long it is. Write the lengths in order from shortest to longest.

1 m | 98 cm | 25 cm | 400 mm

25 cm **400 mm** **98 cm** **1 m**

5 cm | 300 cm | 2 m | 55 mm

5 cm **55 mm** **2 m** **300 cm**

#HAIRGOALS

HINT Convert all the measurements to centimetres before putting them in order. Remember that 100 cm = 1 m and 10 mm = 1 cm.

64

Page 65 — Ordering Capacity

Matching

Moana and Maui collect rainwater as they journey across the ocean. How much water do they collect? Match each measurement in millilitres to its equivalent in litres.

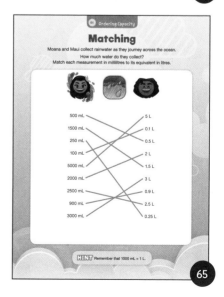

500 mL — 5 L
1500 mL — 0.1 L
250 mL — 0.5 L
100 mL — 2 L
5000 mL — 1.5 L
2000 mL — 3 L
2500 mL — 0.9 L
900 mL — 2.5 L
3000 mL — 0.25 L

HINT Remember that 1000 mL = 1 L.

65

* Sample answers provided.

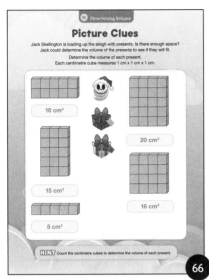

Determining Volume

Picture Clues

Jack Skellington is loading up the sleigh with presents. Is there enough space?
Jack could determine the volume of the presents to see if they will fit.
Determine the volume of each present.
Each centimetre cube measures 1 cm x 1 cm x 1 cm.

10 cm³

20 cm³

15 cm³

16 cm³

5 cm³

HINT Count the centimetre cubes to determine the volume of each present.

66

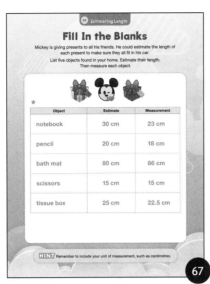

Estimating Length

Fill In the Blanks

Mickey is giving presents to all his friends. He could estimate the length of
each present to make sure they all fit in his car.
List five objects found in your home. Estimate their length.
Then measure each object.

★

Object	Estimate	Measurement
notebook	30 cm	23 cm
pencil	20 cm	18 cm
bath mat	80 cm	86 cm
scissors	15 cm	15 cm
tissue box	25 cm	22.5 cm

HINT Remember to include your unit of measurement, such as centimetres.

67

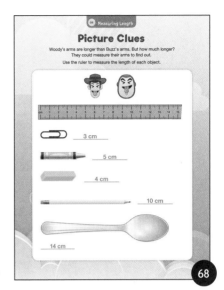

Measuring Length

Picture Clues

Woody's arms are longer than Buzz's arms. But how much longer?
They could measure their arms to find out.
Use the ruler to measure the length of each object.

3 cm

5 cm

4 cm

10 cm

14 cm

68

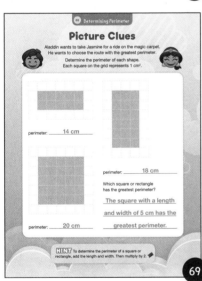

Determining Perimeter

Picture Clues

Aladdin wants to take Jasmine for a ride on the magic carpet.
He wants to choose the route with the greatest perimeter.
Determine the perimeter of each shape.
Each square on the grid represents 1 cm².

perimeter: 14 cm

perimeter: 18 cm

Which square or rectangle
has the greatest perimeter?

The square with a length
and width of 5 cm has the

perimeter: 20 cm   greatest perimeter.

HINT To determine the perimeter of a square or
rectangle, add the length and width. Then multiply by 2.

69

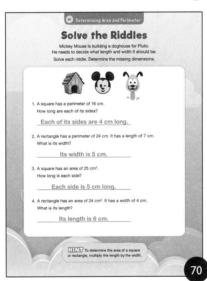

Determining Area and Perimeter

Solve the Riddles

Mickey Mouse is building a doghouse for Pluto.
He needs to decide what length and width it should be.
Solve each riddle. Determine the missing dimensions.

1. A square has a perimeter of 16 cm.
   How long are each of its sides?

   Each of its sides are 4 cm long.

2. A rectangle has a perimeter of 24 cm. It has a length of 7 cm.
   What is its width?

   Its width is 5 cm.

3. A square has an area of 25 cm².
   How long is each side?

   Each side is 5 cm long.

4. A rectangle has an area of 24 cm². It has a width of 4 cm.
   What is its length?

   Its length is 6 cm.

HINT To determine the area of a square
or rectangle, multiply the length by the width.

70

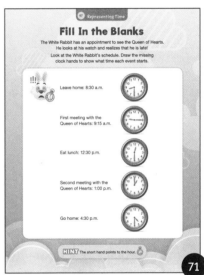

Representing Time

Fill In the Blanks

The White Rabbit has an appointment to see the Queen of Hearts.
He looks at his watch and realizes that he is late!
Look at the White Rabbit's schedule. Draw the missing
clock hands to show what time each event starts.

!!!   Leave home: 8:30 a.m.

First meeting with the
Queen of Hearts: 9:15 a.m.

Eat lunch: 12:30 p.m.

Second meeting with the
Queen of Hearts: 1:00 p.m.

Go home: 4:30 p.m.

HINT The short hand points to the hour.

71

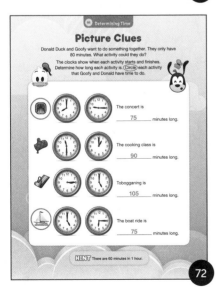

Determining Time

Picture Clues

Donald Duck and Goofy want to do something together. They only have
80 minutes. What activity could they do?
The clocks show when each activity starts and finishes.
Determine how long each activity is. (Circle) each activity
that Goofy and Donald have time to do.

The concert is
75 minutes long.

The cooking class is
90 minutes long.

Tobogganing is
105 minutes long.

The boat ride is
75 minutes long.

HINT There are 60 minutes in 1 hour.

72

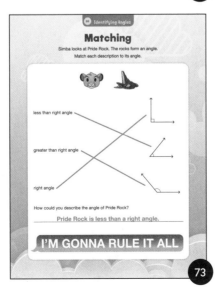

Identifying Angles

Matching

Simba looks at Pride Rock. The rocks form an angle.
Match each description to its angle.

less than right angle

greater than right angle

right angle

How could you describe the angle of Pride Rock?

Pride Rock is less than a right angle.

I'M GONNA RULE IT ALL

73

★ Sample answers provided.

107

Answers

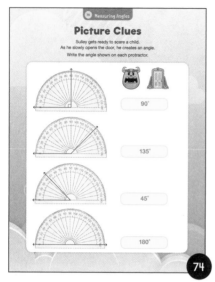

Picture Clues

Sulley gets ready to scare a child.
As he slowly opens the door, he creates an angle.
Write the angle shown on each protractor.

90°

135°

45°

180°

74

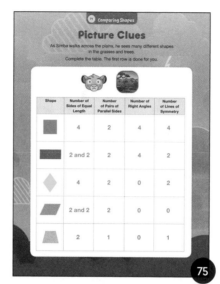

Picture Clues

As Simba walks across the plains, he sees many different shapes
in the grasses and trees.
Complete the table. The first row is done for you.

Shape	Number of Sides of Equal Length	Number of Pairs of Parallel Sides	Number of Right Angles	Number of Lines of Symmetry
	4	2	4	4
	2 and 2	2	4	2
	4	2	0	2
	2 and 2	2	0	0
	2	1	0	1

75

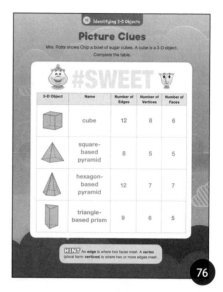

Picture Clues

Mrs. Potts shows Chip a bowl of sugar cubes. A cube is a 3-D object.
Complete the table.

#SWEET

3-D Object	Name	Number of Edges	Number of Vertices	Number of Faces
	cube	12	8	6
	square-based pyramid	8	5	5
	hexagon-based pyramid	12	7	7
	triangle-based prism	9	6	5

HINT An **edge** is where two faces meet. A **vertex** (plural form: **vertices**) is where two or more edges meet.

76

Matching

The magic carpet is hiding from Aladdin. It hides by rolling up into a cylinder.
When it unrolls and lies flat, it is a rectangle.
Match each 3-D object to its net.

77

Fill In the Blanks

Alice is in Wonderland. The playing cards combine to form
3-D objects with edges, vertices, and faces.
Complete the table.

#FUN!!

3-D Object	Name	Number of Edges	Number of Vertices	Number of Faces
	octagon-based prism	24	16	10
	rectangle-based prism	12	8	6
	hexagon-based prism	18	12	8
	pentagon-based prism	15	10	7

HINT You can use the 3-D object flash cards on page 115 to help you.

78

Solve the Riddles

Scuttle thinks he knows a lot about human objects.
But he often doesn't have the right name for them!
Solve each riddle. Write the name of the 3-D object.

1. I have 12 edges and 6 triangle faces.
What 3-D object am I?

   hexagon-based pyramid

2. I have an even number of edges and vertices.
I have 6 rectangle faces.
What 3-D object am I?

   hexagon-based prism

3. I have 8 vertices and 6 faces.
What 3-D object am I?

   cube

Dinglehopper!

79

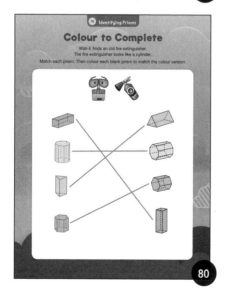

Colour to Complete

Wall-E finds an old fire extinguisher.
The fire extinguisher looks like a cylinder.
Match each prism. Then colour each blank prism to match the colour version.

80

Word Search

Dory is looking everywhere for her parents.
She searches high and she searches low. She is on a fish search!
Complete the word search. Circle the name of each 3-D object.

HELP ME

R U LOST?

SPHERE
CUBE
CYLINDER
PRISM
CONE
PYRAMID
TETRAHEDRON

P	A	J	M	O	S	P	H	E	R	E
Y	D	O	C	W	K	O	A	S	D	N
R	E	L	Y	E	M	P	R	I	S	M
A	P	O	L	T	C	F	A	D	E	N
M	Q	U	I	N	U	Z	C	O	N	E
I	N	O	N	P	B	R	G	K	H	A
D	S	A	D	U	E	Y	E	S	U	D
T	E	S	E	K	A	D	M	W	A	L
T	E	T	R	A	H	E	D	R	O	N
G	W	X	L	O	N	R	A	W	M	M

81

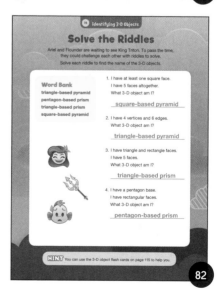

Solve the Riddles

Ariel and Flounder are waiting to see King Triton. To pass the time,
they could challenge each other with riddles to solve.
Solve each riddle to find the name of the 3-D objects.

Word Bank
triangle-based pyramid
pentagon-based prism
triangle-based prism
square-based pyramid

1. I have at least one square face.
I have 5 faces altogether.
What 3-D object am I?

   square-based pyramid

2. I have 4 vertices and 6 edges.
What 3-D object am I?

   triangle-based pyramid

3. I have triangle and rectangle faces.
I have 5 faces.
What 3-D object am I?

   triangle-based prism

4. I have a pentagon base.
I have rectangular faces.
What 3-D object am I?

   pentagon-based prism

HINT You can use the 3-D object flash cards on page 115 to help you.

82

*Sample answers provided.

Matching

83 Sorting 3-D Objects

Rapunzel sees lots of lanterns.
The lanterns are shaped like rectangle-based prisms.
Match each 3-D object with the correct number of vertices.

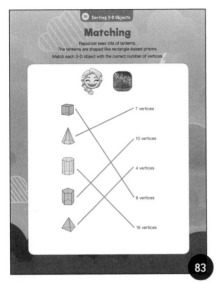

- 7 vertices
- 10 vertices
- 4 vertices
- 8 vertices
- 16 vertices

Picture Clues

84 Identifying Symmetry

The gang from Halloween Town may be scary,
but some them are also symmetrical.
Draw the line of symmetry for each face.

HINT An image is symmetrical when you can draw a line through it and both halves are the same.

Colour to Complete

85 Identifying Symmetry

Maleficent is one of the most fearsome villains around! She has green skin and long horns. Her horns and face are symmetrical.
Colour each picture so that it is symmetrical.

#GOGREEN

Maze

86 Identifying Symmetry

Dory is caught by the jellyfish!
Marlin needs to swim through the jellyfish to reach her.
Find a path through the maze.
Follow the shapes with two or more lines of symmetry.

Start

Finish

Picture Clues

87 Identifying Symmetry

Elsa creates snowflakes with her ice powers. Snowflakes are symmetrical.
Draw the lines of symmetry for each shape.
Write how many lines of symmetry there are.

#ICE!

6 2
4 6
5 3

HINT Trace each shape onto a piece of paper. Cut it out. Fold the paper in half several times. Check for the lines of symmetry.

Picture Clues

88 Identifying Transformations

At Monsters, Inc., they do not scare children anymore. They make them laugh instead! Sulley looks in the mirror to practise making funny faces. His image is reflected.
Decide whether each image is a translation, rotation, or reflection.

#FUNNY

The image is a ___ reflection

The image is a ___ translation

The image is a ___ rotation

HINT **Translation** means "a slide." **Rotation** means "a turn." **Reflection** means "a flip."

Matching

89 Identifying Transformations

Anna and Elsa are exploring the castle. They find a trunk.
They look inside. It's full of winter clothes.
Match each pair of images to the correct name for the transformation.

SISTERS!

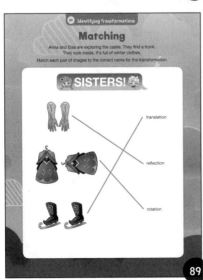

- translation
- reflection
- rotation

Picture Clues

90 Identifying Location

The toys are scattered across Andy's room.
Woody could create a map to show where each toy is located.
Use the map to answer each question.

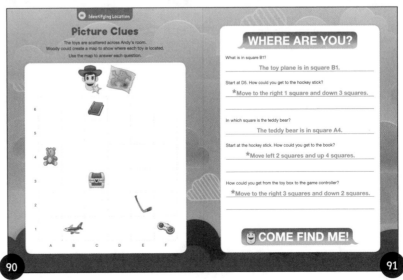

WHERE ARE YOU?

What is in square B1?
The toy plane is in square B1.

Start at D5. How could you get to the hockey stick?
*Move to the right 1 square and down 3 squares.

In which square is the teddy bear?
The teddy bear is in square A4.

Start at the hockey stick. How could you get to the book?
*Move left 2 squares and up 4 squares.

How could you get from the toy box to the game controller?
*Move to the right 3 squares and down 2 squares.

😊 COME FIND ME!

*Sample answers provided.

Answers

Picture Clues

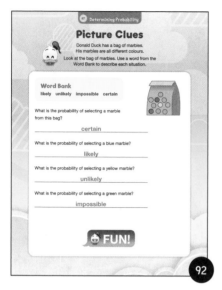

Donald Duck has a bag of marbles.
His marbles are all different colours.
Look at the bag of marbles. Use a word from the
Word Bank to describe each situation.

Word Bank
likely unlikely impossible certain

What is the probability of selecting a marble
from this bag?
certain

What is the probability of selecting a blue marble?
likely

What is the probability of selecting a yellow marble?
unlikely

What is the probability of selecting a green marble?
impossible

😊 FUN!

92

Picture Clues

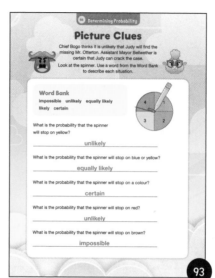

Chief Bogo thinks it is unlikely that Judy will find the
missing Mr. Otterton. Assistant Mayor Bellwether is
certain that Judy can crack the case.
Look at the spinner. Use a word from the Word Bank
to describe each situation.

Word Bank
impossible unlikely equally likely
likely certain

What is the probability that the spinner
will stop on yellow?
unlikely

What is the probability that the spinner will stop on blue or yellow?
equally likely

What is the probability that the spinner will stop on a colour?
certain

What is the probability that the spinner will stop on red?
unlikely

What is the probability that the spinner will stop on brown?
impossible

93

Colour to Complete

Genie grants nearly all wishes. There are only three wishes he cannot grant.
It is likely that Aladdin's wishes will be granted.
Colour the gumballs to match each situation.

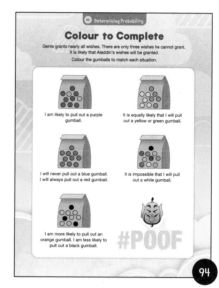

I am likely to pull out a purple gumball.

It is equally likely that I will pull out a yellow or green gumball.

I will never pull out a blue gumball. I will always pull out a red gumball.

It is impossible that I will pull out a white gumball.

I am more likely to pull out an orange gumball. I am less likely to pull out a black gumball.

#POOF

94

Picture Clues

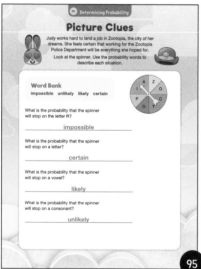

Judy works hard to land a job in Zootopia, the city of her
dreams. She feels certain that working for the Zootopia
Police Department will be everything she hoped for.
Look at the spinner. Use the probability words to
describe each situation.

Word Bank
impossible unlikely likely certain

What is the probability that the spinner
will stop on the letter R?
impossible

What is the probability that the spinner
will stop on a letter?
certain

What is the probability that the spinner
will stop on a vowel?
likely

What is the probability that the spinner
will stop on a consonant?
unlikely

95

Graphing

Arendelle gets a lot of precipitation. In places that get a lot of precipitation,
people record how much rain or snow falls.
Read the data shown in the tally chart.

What do you notice about the data in this tally chart?
***More rain fell in June than March.**

Month	Precipitation in cm
January	𝍷𝍷𝍷𝍷 𝍷𝍷 𝍷𝍷
February	𝍷𝍷𝍷𝍷 𝍷𝍷𝍷𝍷 𝍷𝍷
March	𝍷𝍷𝍷𝍷 𝍷𝍷𝍷𝍷
April	𝍷𝍷𝍷𝍷 𝍷𝍷𝍷𝍷
May	𝍷𝍷𝍷𝍷 𝍷𝍷𝍷𝍷 𝍷𝍷𝍷𝍷 𝍷𝍷
June	𝍷𝍷𝍷𝍷 𝍷𝍷𝍷𝍷 𝍷𝍷𝍷𝍷 𝍷𝍷𝍷𝍷 𝍷𝍷 𝍷𝍷𝍷

Use the data in the tally chart to create a bar graph.
Think about the title, headings, and labels. What
interval will you use?

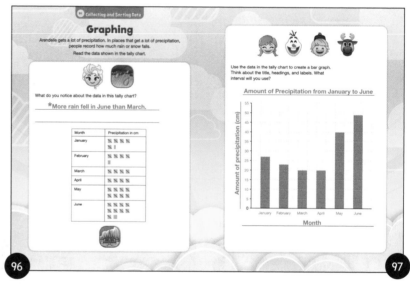

Amount of Precipitation from January to June

(bar graph: y-axis "Amount of precipitation (cm)", x-axis "Month" with January through June)

96 **97**

Fill In the Blanks

Mickey Mouse sees snowflakes everywhere!
What is the median number of snowflakes he sees?
Write each set of numbers in order. Then determine the median.

70 50 65 52 89
50 **52** **65** **69** **70**
Median: **65**

115 112 111 119 108 121 125
108 **111** **112** **115** **119** **121** **125**
Median: **115**

1025 1011 1276 1272 1188 1165 1347
1011 **1025** **1165** **1188** **1272** **1276** **1347**
Median: **1188**

HINT To find the median, first arrange the numbers from
least to greatest. Then look for the number in the middle.

98

Matching

Alice is stuck in Wonderland. She wonders if everything that is happening
is real or if she is in the middle of a dream.
Match each set of numbers to the correct median.

😊 HUH?

8 47 29 11 38 58 25   62
843 145 440 696 828   150
38 62 61 92 99 5 88   80
189 468 532 580 436 888   500
94 41 75 25 97 85   696
192 140 195 160 124 116   29

R U DREAMING?

HINT The **median** is the number in the middle of a set of numbers arranged from least
to greatest. If there are two numbers in the middle, add them together and divide by two.

99

110

Learning Tools

1	2	3	4	5	6	7	8	9	10
11	12	13	14	15	16	17	18	19	20
21	22	23	24	25	26	27	28	29	30
31	32	33	34	35	36	37	38	39	40
41	42	43	44	45	46	47	48	49	50
51	52	53	54	55	56	57	58	59	60
61	62	63	64	65	66	67	68	69	70
71	72	73	74	75	76	77	78	79	80
81	82	83	84	85	86	87	88	89	90
91	92	93	94	95	96	97	98	99	100

×	1	2	3	4	5	6	7	8	9	10
1	1	2	3	4	5	6	7	8	9	10
2	2	4	6	8	10	12	14	16	18	20
3	3	6	9	12	15	18	21	24	27	30
4	4	8	12	16	20	24	28	32	36	40
5	5	10	15	20	25	30	35	40	45	50
6	6	12	18	24	30	36	42	48	54	60
7	7	14	21	28	35	42	49	56	63	70
8	8	16	24	32	40	48	56	64	72	80
9	9	18	27	36	45	54	63	72	81	90
10	10	20	30	40	50	60	70	80	90	100

Thousands	Hundreds	Tens	Ones

Cut out these flash cards. You can use them to learn more about 3-D objects.

Name: square-based pyramid

Vertices: 5

Edges: 8

Faces: 5

Name: triangle-based prism

Vertices: 6

Edges: 9

Faces: 5

Name: triangle-based pyramid

Vertices: 4

Edges: 6

Faces: 4

Name: rectangle-based prism

Vertices: 8

Edges: 12

Faces: 6

Name: rectangle-based pyramid

Vertices: 5

Edges: 8

Faces: 5

Name: cube

Vertices: 8

Edges: 12

Faces: 6

Name: hexagon-based prism

Vertices: 12

Edges: 18

Faces: 8

Name: hexagon-based pyramid

Vertices: 7

Edges: 12

Faces: 7

Name: pentagon-based prism

Vertices: 10

Edges: 15

Faces: 7

Cut out these flash cards. You can use them to learn more about 3-D objects.

Congratulations

_____!

Print your name.

You have finished the
Brain Boost learning path.
Way to go!